Roman History

This is a volume in the Arno Press collection

ROMAN HISTORY

Advisory Editor
T. James Luce, Jr.

Editorial Board
Timothy D. Barnes
Erich S. Gruen
Jerzy Linderski

*See last pages of this volume
for a complete list of titles.*

ROMAN POLICY IN EPIRUS AND ACARNANIA IN THE AGE OF THE ROMAN CONQUEST OF GREECE

Stewart Irvin Oost

ARNO PRESS
A New York Times Company
New York — 1975

Editorial Supervision: MARIE STARECK

Reprint Edition 1975 by Arno Press Inc.

Copyright 1954 by Southern Methodist
   University Press
Reprinted by permission of Southern
   Methodist University Press

ROMAN HISTORY
ISBN for complete set: 0-405-07177-9
See last pages of this volume for titles.

Manufactured in the United States of America

Library of Congress Cataloging in Publication Data

Oost, Stewart Irvin, 1922-
   Roman policy in Epirus and Acarnania in the age of
the Roman conquest of Greece.

   (Roman history)
   Reprint of the ed. published by Southern Methodist University Press, Dallas, which was issued as v. 4 of Arnold Foundation studies, new ser.
   1. Epirus--History. 2. Aitolia kai Akarnania, Greece--History. 3. Rome--Foreign relations. 4. Greece--History--146 B.C.-323 A.D. I. Title. II. Series. III. Series: Arnold Foundation studies ; new ser., v. 4.
[DF261.E65O55 1975] 938'.2   75-7333
ISBN 0-405-07050-0

ROMAN POLICY IN EPIRUS AND ACARNANIA IN THE AGE OF THE ROMAN CONQUEST OF GREECE

Stewart Irvin Oost

ARNOLD FOUNDATION STUDIES

VOLUME IV, NEW SERIES

DALLAS
SOUTHERN METHODIST UNIVERSITY PRESS
1954

COPYRIGHT 1954 BY

SOUTHERN METHODIST UNIVERSITY PRESS

LIBRARY OF CONGRESS CATALOG CARD NUMBER: 54-8702

PRINTED IN THE UNITED STATES OF AMERICA

AT DALLAS, TEXAS

PREFACE

THIS STUDY proposes to make clear the main lines of Rome's policy toward two states which happened to be so situated geographically that they assumed more than ordinary importance for a power extending its influence over the southern Balkan peninsula from the west. Roman policy did not act upon Epirus and Acarnania in a vacuum; hence it has been necessary also to trace some aspects of the foreign policy of these two states in the Hellenistic world of the third century, in order to understand the situation upon which the Romans obtruded themselves. It has also been found necessary from time to time to discuss the general interpretation of Roman imperialism in the east. This is particularly true of Roman policy at the beginning of the Second Macedonian War.

The sources for such a study are quite scanty. They are almost exclusively literary, Polybius and Livy for the most part; and the attention of the ancient historians was rightly centered upon the protagonists of the action, Rome and Macedonia, or Rome and Antiochus. In addition, Livy is primarily interested in Rome and in matters with a direct bearing on her history, while Polybius is reduced to scattered fragments, frequently at crucial points. Conjecture and inference, therefore, play a large part in what follows. I have tried to indicate carefully where the evidence leaves off and the conjectures and inferences of others, as well as my own, begin.

My debts to others are very great. In addition to the obligations mentioned in the footnotes I should especially record here my indebtedness to the published works of Maurice Holleaux, J. A. O. Larsen, F. W. Walbank, and Gaetano de Sanctis. Their services in elucidating the whole general problem of Roman eastern imperialism in the middle Republic, as well as their clarification of many particular points, render possible whatever services an essay such as this, devoted to studying certain side-issues, may be able to perform.

I am very happy to have an opportunity to thank some of the persons who helped in various ways in the preparation of this essay. I wish to thank Professors Herbert Gambrell and Francis Ballard of Southern Methodist University for allowing me to arrange my academic schedule so as to provide opportunities for work of this kind. Professor Carl Roebuck of Northwestern University has made a number of useful suggestions for the betterment of this study. My greatest debt of gratitude is to Professor J. A. O. Larsen, who first revealed to me that even Mommsen could be wrong, who suggested this topic of investigation, and who, in the midst of academic and scholarly burdens even greater than usual, patiently read this essay and gave it the benefit of many valuable criticisms.

CONTENTS

PREFACE v

I. INTRODUCTION: EPIRUS AND ACARNANIA IN THE
   MIDDLE OF THE THIRD CENTURY B.C. 1

II. THE FIRST MACEDONIAN WAR: FROM INDIFFERENCE
    TO *AMICITIA* 16

III. THE SECOND MACEDONIAN AND SYRIAN WARS:
     AMICITIA AND CONCILIATION 40

IV. THE THIRD MACEDONIAN WAR: DOMINATION . . . 68

APPENDIX: THE ALLEGED ACARNANIAN APPEAL TO ROME . 92

NOTES 98

Chapter I

INTRODUCTION: EPIRUS AND ACARNANIA IN THE MIDDLE OF THE THIRD CENTURY B. C.

ANY POWER DESIRING TO INTERFERE in the affairs of the Balkans from bases in the Italian peninsula to the west must obviously direct its attention particularly to the coastal regions and the islands immediately opposite Italy. In antiquity this region was occupied by Illyrian tribes, more or less united at various times in their history. But in ancient times, at least, because of the tortured conformation of the mountains just behind the Illyrian coast, the best and easiest route eastward and southward necessitated a sharp turn from Illyria to the southeast. In this direction the Aous valley provides comparatively easy passes, albeit narrow and twisting,[1] which conduct the invader eventually to the seat of ancient Greek civilization to the south, and by a circuitous route afford in the end the easiest way to approach ancient Macedonia itself. This was a lesson which the Romans learned in 199 B.C., when their general Galba tried in vain to traverse the direct route through Illyria across the main Pindus range. This direct route thereafter was employed, before the construction of the Egnatian Way, only in the Syrian War (191 and 190 B.C.), when a friendly Macedonian government helped to solve the difficult problems of logistics involved.

Accordingly the Roman government, when it became involved in Greek affairs, had a particular interest in Epirus, through which the easier southeastern route ran. Moreover, a friendly or at least a not actively hostile Acarnania, to the south of Epirus, would secure Roman communications and supply lines through the ports around the Ambracian Gulf, notably Ambracia itself. The coast of Epirus has no really good harbors at all. But the route through Epirus had first to be brought under control to prevent a possible northern flanking maneuver against those supply lines in the Ambracian Gulf. In addition, ancient naval policy was conditioned by ships which sailed from headland to headland and which put in often to revictual. Such circumstances obviously required that the coast line along which the warships and supply ships were to sail should not, at least at strategic intervals, be in the hands of actively hostile powers.[2] The waters off Acarnania comprised a crucial stretch in the voyage for Roman ships sailing eastward. After the jump across the open sea from Italy to the Balkan coast, even with bases on the Greek islands off that coast, the Romans would be hampered by a policy of hostility pursued by a power which controlled the land past which the ships must sail on their further journey: either south around the Peloponnese, or eastward into the Corinthian Gulf, or into the Ambracian Gulf to the city of Ambracia, behind which lay a direct but steep route eastward into Thessaly.

Acarnania and Epirus, therefore, enjoyed a peculiar relationship to Italy, geographically speaking. An attempt will be made below to show that to some degree Roman policy toward those two states differed somewhat from Roman policy toward the Greeks of the Greek homeland generally.[3] It seems likely that these differences of policy were based upon tactical and strategic considerations, which in turn arose from the geographical factors sketched above.

These two states, Epirus and Acarnania, had played a relatively insignificant role in Greek history. Neither had ever been a great power in the Greek world, unless Epirus be so counted in the reign of the great Pyrrhus (died 272 B.C.). The Acarnanians in the late fifth and fourth centuries B.C. had adhered closely to a policy of alliance with Athens — until, in the last decades of the fourth century, they switched their allegiance to the new great power, Macedonia.[4] Epirus, too, in the later fourth century was usually a satellite of Macedonia, until Pyrrhus I was able to profit by his own abilities — and the calamities which beset Macedonia in the opening years of the third century — to act independently.

At virtually no time throughout all the history of Epirus as an independent state were the various tribes of which it was composed ever completely amalgamated into a unified people. At all stages of their history we find the tribes acting separately; even in the last rash struggle they opposed only divided councils to Roman control. Fourteen of these tribes were known to Theopompus in the fourth century B.C.[5] and it is quite possible that there were more.[6] But of the many Epirote tribes three were by far the most important: Chaonians, Thesprotians, and Molossians. These three tribes at various times dominated Epirus, but by the later fourth century the Molossians had won ascendancy over their rivals. The royal house was Molossian; Pyrrhus I, although king of all Epirus and more, boasted proudly of his Molossian lineage.[7] Epirus, moreover, generally speaking was far behind most of Greece in culture and civilization as late as the middle of the second century B.C. It had few cities properly so-called; the seventy "cities" destroyed in 167 B.C. must have been mainly villages.[8] Stock raising and animal husbandry seem to have been a specialty of the country,[9] whose principal way of life must have been rural.

Epirus enjoyed one comparatively brief flash of glory under her great king, Pyrrhus I, in the first quarter of the third century. In addition to parts of adjacent Illyria and, from time to time, of Macedonia, Pyrrhus extended his sway over Acarnania.[10] That country, too, while not so backward as Epirus — largely because of its greater proximity to the principal centers of Hellenic civilization — did not as a whole present the typical characteristics of classical Greek urbanization until a relatively late period. Cassander, king of Macedonia at the end of the fourth century, seems to have played a large part in furthering the urbanization of Acarnania.[11] In all probability Acarnania was a region of large cattle ranches only in less degree than was Epirus.[12]

The power of Epirus did not long survive the death of Pyrrhus I in 272 B.C. Pyrrhus was succeeded by his son, Alexander II, who saw almost at once the beginning of the break-up of his father's dominions. The Illyrians attacked the new king from the north while, perhaps taking advantage of this diversion, the Acarnanians to the south renounced their connection with Epirus.[13]

But the independence of the Acarnanians was short-lived. To the east of Acarnania lay the Aetolian League or Federation. The Aetolians had been involved in intermittent hostilities with the Acarnanians for centuries, and in the middle of the third century, when the Aetolians were making great strides in extending their federal state in all directions, the Acarnanians had especial reason to be anxious. Besides, the Acarnanians may well have feared an attempt by Alexander to resubject them to his authority. If so, the event proved such fears well grounded. On the other hand, an independent Acarnania which might return to its old alliance with Macedonia constituted a threat to Aetolia.[14] The first solution found to the problem, a solution probably quite satisfactory to the Acarnanians, was the conclusion of a treaty of friendship between Aetolia and Acarnania. The boundary between the two powers, frequently a source of contention in the past, was to be the river Achelous "as far as the sea," excepting two places.[15] There were to be mutual rights of intermarriage, ownership of land, and isopolity,[16] as well as mutual assistance in time of defensive war.[17] The treaty was typical of the kind used by the Aetolians to spread their influence, but unhappily it shortly proved a dead letter. The next known event in the history of Acarnania is an agreement between Alexander II of Epirus and the Aetolians to partition Acarnania between them. One can only conclude that both Alexander and the Aetolians had agreed that half was better than none. Acarnania was thereupon divided between them; the northwestern half with Leucas and Medion probably going to Alexander, the southern and eastern half with the principal cities of Stratus, Phoetiae, Oeniadae, and Metropolis to Aetolia.[18]

Unfortunately, the chronology of these events is quite obscure. They fall after the death of Pyrrhus and during the reign of Alexander II, and obviously must have occurred in this order. The usual dating of the Aetolian-Acarnanian treaty has been to the years immediately following the death of Pyrrhus, but recently arguments have been advanced for a date approximately a decade later.[19] At any rate, for the time being Acarnania as a separate political entity disappeared from the map of Greece.[20] If their subsequent history is any argument, the Acarnanians bore a much deeper grudge against the Aetolians than against the Epirotes. After all, they had only recently separated from Epirus and might regard as inevitable an attempt to reannex them; but their treaty with Aetolia had been violated with a completely Machiavellian lack of principle. Since in the future it would be extremely unwise for an independent Acarnania to be hostile to both of her most important neighbors, when a portion of the Acarnanians regained their independence about 230 B.C. they chose as their friend Epirus, against whom they bore the least resentment and from whose aggression they had least to fear.

The decline of the monarchy under the successors of Pyrrhus

continued apace in Epirus. Alexander II unwisely saw in Antigonus Gonatas' difficulties in the Chremonidean War an opportunity to attack Macedonia. Demetrius, son of Antigonus, not only expelled Alexander from Macedonia, but drove him out of Epirus for a time as well.[21] After the death of Alexander still further misfortunes befell Epirus and its monarchy. Alexander probably died, it seems fairly well agreed, about 240 B.C.[22] His sister-wife, Olympias, regent of Epirus after his death, was forced to appeal to Demetrius, king of Macedonia, for aid against the Aetolians, who were trying to seize the Epirote half of Acarnania. The accord arrived at between the two monarchies was sealed by the marriage of Olympias' daughter, Phthia, to Demetrius.[23] Olympias and her two sons, Pyrrhus II and Ptolemy, died shortly thereafter in quick succession.[24] The sole survivors of the Epirote royal house were Nereis, daughter of the great Pyrrhus and wife of the Syracusan prince, Gelo, and her sister Deidameia. Thus the royal family in Epirus was reduced to one representative, Deidameia.[25] Her tenure of royal power was destined to be very short.

It is well known that by the third century before Christ the economic-social question in the Greek world, posed by the fact that the rich were getting richer and the poor poorer, was becoming acute.[26] It seems likely that such conditions prevailed in Epirus (and Acarnania), as it is known they did in nearby Aetolia. This factor, combined probably with the incompetence of the Epirote monarchs after Pyrrhus I and the fact, or rumor, of dark crimes responsible for the sudden deaths of members of the royal family,[27] provoked an insurrection which overthrew Deidameia, who lost her life through treachery as well.[28]

Happily we are not entirely dependent on applying generalizations from the rest of Greece to Epirus to show that this revolution was, at least in part, an episode in class strife. Justin[29] seems to imply that a socio-economic factor was involved in the revolution when he says that the gods took vengeance for the impiety of the murder of Deidameia, which occurred in a shrine; for the Epirotes were "et sterilitatem famemque passi et intestina discordia vexati." The Epirotes suffered hunger and barrenness (possibly poverty) and were harassed by civil strife. Inasmuch as a more skeptical age may doubt that the gods did actually punish the sacrilege, perhaps this can be taken as a general description of the condition of Epirus in what we may pretentiously call its "revolutionary epoch." Even more significant is the language of Pausanias:[30] τά τε ἄλλα ὁ δῆμος ὕβριζε καὶ ἀκροᾶσθαι τῶν ἐν ταῖς ἀρχαῖς ὑπερεώρων The (common) people committed *hybris* and disobeyed the magistrates. These two statements of late and inferior sources would mean little if taken by themselves, but in view of what is known about conditions elsewhere in Greece they confirm the suspicion that the fall of the Aeacidae was merely the most obvious symptom of socio-economic discontent in Epirus.

We cannot date the revolution in Epirus with exactitude, but it probably occurred about 233 B.C.[31] The new government of Epirus seems not to have differed markedly from the old. The Epirotes had been organized as a federal *koinon* under their kings, a sympolity which nevertheless referred to itself as a symmachy. After the revolution the Epirotes retained their federal organization. Instead of the king, however, the league was headed by three *strategoi*,[32] but only one seems to have been eponymous;[33] hence it has been surmised that one of the three *strategoi* ranked above the other two.[34] The league had the usual assembly with the usual powers over war, peace, alliance, embassies, and so on. There was also a *synedrion* which exercised probouleutic functions. The new government had its seat at Phoenice in Chaonia, rather than at Ambracia where the capital had been since the days of Pyrrhus I.[35]

More important than the mechanical structure of the government was its general character after the revolution; that is to say, in the era of Roman intervention in Greece. In the Hellenistic age true democracy in the fifth-century classical sense, or in the sense ordinarily attached to the word in the West at present, was comparatively rare. There is strong reason for believing that even the word "democracy" had come in the Hellenistic age merely to describe a nonmonarchical form of government.[36] Certainly after the revolution Epirus was a democracy in that sense; was it a democracy in any more liberal sense of the word? It would afford a quite surprising example to the student of Hellenistic political institutions if it were. Unhappily our sources do not permit us to apply the usual tests — pay for magistrates and councilors, or the lack of it; limitation of the assembly to a small number, and so on. There is, however, one circumstance which may be construed to mean that the government of Epirus was an oligarchy of some sort; that is to say, that the "better" classes controlled the government. A famous episode in Hellenistic history is the treacherous seizure of Phoenice, center of the *koinon,* by the Illyrians in 230 B.C. The Illyrian pounce upon the city was facilitated by the perfidy of a band of Gallic mercenaries in Epirote employ.[37] These Gauls formed a garrison for the city of Phoenice, but Polybius calls them more than that; the Epirotes made the Gauls the τῆς δημοκρατίας καὶ τῶν νόμων φύλακας, "the guards of their democracy and their laws."[38] In the first place Polybius refers to Epirus as a δημοκρατ α and we have seen that the use of this word in the Hellenistic age need make it no more than a synonym for oligarchy. But in addition the government finds it necessary to employ mercenaries to protect the prevailing regime. It is difficult, therefore, to avoid the conclusion that the government of Epirus in 230 was not a popular one. The internal safety of the "democracy" was assured by hirelings. Hence it seems fairly reasonable to assume that Epirus formed no exception to the general political trend of the Hellenistic world. We have also seen that Epirus in the "revolutionary era" was considerably convulsed by internecine strife. The presence of this mercenary guard at the seat of government is thus explained; and if the reasoning outlined above is correct, we must conclude that after the period of social and civil discord the "upper" classes had won control again. In the events of the year 230, as described by Polybius, we see no evidence of renewed civil commotion in Epirus. Polybius' strictures on the laxity of the Epirotes regarding foreign foes, and the Illyrians in particular, relate equally well to the people and to the government.[39]

One of the purposes of Antigonus Doson's Hellenic League, which the Epirotes joined a few years later, was the combating of social revolution, for the king announced that he was making war, not upon Sparta, but upon Cleomenes, its radical sovereign.[40] Accordingly we may assume that not the least of the motives which led Epirus to join the Hellenic League was the interest of its oligarchy in offering resistance to social revolution.

An important result of these disturbances in Epirus, whether the overthrow of the monarchy or its difficulties in the last decade of its existence, was the loss of a number of outlying possessions. Acarnania, or rather that portion of it which Alexander II had seized, became independent once again.[41] The new government was made a federal state in typical Hellenistic fashion and probably with an organization very similar to what it had had in previous periods of independence in the late fourth and third centuries. Leucas became the seat of the government; at least it was the capital in 197.[42] At the head of the government was a *strategos*, and the structure of the state included a *synedrion* or council as well as an assembly known as "The Thousand."[43] Obviously, then, Acarnania was an oligarchy, since its assembly was limited to a thousand members more or less, it not being necessary to take the figure literally. Very possibly, in typical moderate oligarchic fashion "The Thousand" represented a hoplite franchise.[44] We may therefore assume that the new government of Acarnania, like that of Epirus, would be interested in repressing social revolution and may equally well have joined Antigonus Doson's Hellenic League partly on that account.

Acarnania was not the only territory lost to the Epirotes. The city of Ambracia, the capital under the monarchy,[45] was probably lost about 230. In 219 it certainly belonged to the Aetolians;[46] hence the most likely time for it to have been lost to Epirus is the period of disorder and confusion attendant upon the overthrow of the monarchy.[47] In addition, the loss of Ambracia almost certainly means that Amphilochia was lost at the same time to Aetolia, or shortly before, inasmuch as Amphilochia lies between Ambracia and the territories of the Aetolian League.[48]

In the last decade of its existence the Epirote royal family had been allied with Macedonia, the Epirote princess Phthia being the queen of Demetrius II. The overthrow of the monarchy in Epirus and the treacherous murder of its last representative there naturally meant the estrangement of Macedonia. Hence when Epirus needed help, as she did in 230, her government turned to the Aetolians and Achaeans for aid. It has been usual to suppose that the Epirote revolution was supported, if not incited, by the Aetolians who saw in it a means of depriving Macedonia of an ally.[49] This is not at all impossible, but it is only an inference. The rupture of friendly relations with Macedonia almost certainly must have followed the murder of Deidameia, however.[50] Accordingly, if the Epirotes were to need help in the near future they could not expect it from the court of Pella. Events more famous for introducing an almost new factor into Greek politics soon caused the Epirotes to look for external assistance.

Acarnania[51] had hardly won its independence from Epirus when the Aetolians attempted to realize their ancient ambition to add their western neighbors to their league. Diplomacy failing to attain this object,[52] the Aetolians laid seige to the Acarnanian city of Medion. Possibly even before the Aetolians had laid seige to the city, the people of Medion, anticipating such a move, sent an appeal to Demetrius of Macedonia for aid.[53] Demetrius, his hands full with war against both the northern barbarians and the Achaean and Aetolian Leagues, bribed Agron, king of Illyria, to relieve Medion. The Illyrian monarch sailed southward with an Illyrian force of five thousand aboard a fleet of a hundred *lemboi,* the light, fast-sailing Illyrian corsair ships. Landing in secrecy, he fell suddenly upon the Aetolians encamped before Medion, and with some assistance from the citizens of the town routed the invader. Thereupon the Illyrians returned home with large booty.[54] During the subsequent winter (231/0) Agron died and the administration of the kingdom devolved upon his wife, Teuta. The next spring Teuta, emboldened by her subjects' defeat of the foremost military power of Greece, sent out a new expedition whose purpose was organized piracy. After raiding Elis and Messenia, the Illyrians put in at the Epirote capital Phoenice[55] to revictual. Here they fell in with congenial spirits, the force of some eight hundred Gallic mercenaries entrusted with the defense of the city and of the oligarchic government, which was still uneasy about the tumults that had occurred during the recent revolution. With the treasonable assistance of this Gallic band, which was long accustomed to feats of this sort,[56] the Illyrians seized the town. Upon the intelligence of this disaster, the native Epirotes hastily mobilized to oppose the Illyrians, but were compelled to divide their forces in order to protect the city of Antigoneia in Atintania, the chief entrance to Epirus from the north, for another Illyrian force under command of the Illyrian chieftain Scerdilaidas was approaching by land in this direction. The Epirote force confronting the pirates at Phoenice was ignominiously trounced.[57]

The Epirotes now looked about for aid and sent ambassadors to the Achaean and Aetolian Leagues, which agreed to assist against the Illyrians. Possibly treaties of alliance were drawn up with both Achaea and Aetolia;[58] in any event a relieving force was dispatched by the two leagues forthwith. Yet before battle could be joined, the Illyrians were called home to quell a revolt. After pillaging the country the marauders made a truce with the Epirotes; Phoenice was surrendered with its free inhabitants, but the slaves and other property were carried away to Illyria.[59]

The Illyrians had long engaged in piracy in the Adriatic, but never before on such a scale as this,[60] and their new exploits filled all the peoples of the western coast of Greece with consternation.[61] The Epirotes, bearing in mind that they had signed only a truce with the Illyrians, and evidently not too favorably impressed with the efforts of the two leagues to relieve the Illyrian menace, entered into diplomatic negotiations with Teuta to obtain a lasting peace. The price exacted by the Illyrian government was probably the cession of Atintania, *i.e.* the gorges of the river Aous where the city of Antigoneia guarded the route southward into Epirus and the heart of Greece.[62] In addition the Epirotes went over to the side they believed had the strongest battalions and allied themselves with the Illyrians, engaging to cooperate against the Achaeans and Aetolians. At about the same time the Acarnanians also entered into an alliance with Illyria on the same terms.[63] Particularly since the alliances were directed against Aetolia and Achaea, enemies of Demetrius II, the action of the two powers was a move toward Macedonia, which was allied with Illyria.

In the general history of Greece and of the ancient world as a whole the Illyrian raid on Phoenice had much more important results. The commerce between Magna Graecia and the Greek homeland was centuries old; but in the course of the first half of the third century most of the Greek cities in southern Italy had come under the influence of Rome in one way or another. Rome was therefore bound to protect them. Moreover, by the middle of the third century (if not before) the Italian allies and subjects of Rome seem also to have been taking some part in trans-Adriatic commerce.[64] An important link in the voyage eastward was the stretch across the Adriatic from southern Italy to the coasts of the Greek peninsula. Here the Illyrian pirates had long formed a menace to peaceful navigation, nor had ships from Italy been exempt from their attacks.[65] Ships sailing eastward from Brundisium must have found it convenient to stop at Corcyra on their way south from Apollonia or Epidamnus. Likewise ships approaching Greek waters from the Tarentine Gulf, or still farther west, would naturally make for Corcyra. A glance at the map as well as the subsequent history of Roman warfare in Greece shows that Corcyra was an important port of call for western Greece.[66] The city and port of Corcyra face on the channel which separates the island from the Epirote mainland.[67] An ancient ship would ordinarily round the northern headlands of the island into the strait, only two miles wide at its narrowest. The Italian traders thus would sail past Phoenice — of which they must have had some knowledge, since the city was only a few miles inland from the coast — and past the Epirote town of Buthrotum to the Corcyraean harbor. At the time of the Illyrian attack on Phoenice some of the pirates diverted their attention to the Italian merchants traveling in this region. A successful raid netted them booty in both merchandise and prisoners, and many Italian traders were slain.[68]

The Roman senate had long tolerated these outrages, but at the representations of a number of interested persons on this occasion it dispatched an embassy to expostulate with Teuta in late summer or autumn, 230.[69] It is well known how Teuta refused any satisfaction to the Roman envoys and took considerable umbrage at the freedom of speech used by one of them. When this undiplomatic envoy was assassinated on his homeward journey, rightly or wrongly Teuta was credited with the responsibility for the deed, and the outraged Roman government prepared to go to war.[70]

Notwithstanding the black outlook beyond the Adriatic, the next spring (229) Teuta fitted out another piratical expedition which nearly seized Epidamnus, and then laid seige to Corcyra. The Corcyraeans and the Epidamnians were joined by the Apollonians in sending for help to Achaea and Aetolia. Aid was granted, but the two leagues suffered an ignominious defeat at the hands of the Illyrians off the little island of Paxos a few miles south of Corcyra. In despair thereupon Corcyra surrendered and the Illyrians sailed off to lay siege to Epidamnus.[71] At the battle of Paxos the Acarnanians lived up faithfully to the alliance they had entered upon with the Illyrians the preceding year and contributed seven decked ships to the Illyrian fleet.[72]

Shortly thereafter the Roman fleet, two hundred strong, commanded by the consul, Cn. Fulvius, and a Roman expeditionary force of twenty thousand foot and two thousand horse with the other consul in command arrived in the Balkans.[73] It is not necessary here to recount the events of the First Illyrian War. By the end of the campaigning season Teuta had been completely cowed and in the spring of 228 B.C. she was compelled to agree to peace on Roman terms. During the course of the war the following cities and tribes had gone over to the Roman side: Corcyra, Apollonia, Epidamnus, Issa, the Parthinians, the Atintanians,[74] and Pharos,[75] as well as the Illyrian chieftain, Demetrius of Pharos, who was rewarded with a considerable principality. Oricus is also to be added in all probability,[76] but even so it is quite likely that the list is incomplete.[77]

The terms of the peace treaty after the war are briefly given by Polybius,[78] with further details in Appian.[79] Polybius says that by the terms of the treaty Teuta consented to pay any indemnity[80] imposed, and promised not to sail beyond the promontory of Lissus (*i.e.*, into southern Adriatic and Ionian waters, including the seaway from Italy to Greece) with more than two unarmed vessels. Appian adds that the Romans told the Illyrian ambassadors that Corcyra, Pharos, Issa, Epidamnus, and the Atintanians were already Roman subjects.[81] Pinnes, the minor in whose name Teuta ruled, was to become a friend of the Roman people if he accepted these provisions. In other words, the kingdom of Pinnes was granted a treaty of friendship with Rome.

On the other hand, the treaty in effect ended the alliance which the Illyrians had concluded with the Epirotes and the Acarnanians less than two years before. Since the Illyrians were forbidden to send armed fleets south of Lissus, they could bring the Acarnanians and Epirotes no help by sea. True, there was no provision made, so far as we know, on the subject of Illyrian land forces marching southward; but the specialty of the Illyrians had always been lightning raids by sea — their forces landed to strike at some place on or near the coast, and then retired. Moreover, the particular objects against which the alliance had been directed were the Achaean and Aetolian Leagues. But these leagues were now placed effectively out of the reach of the Illyrians, who would thus be in no need of assistance against them from the Epirotes or the

Acarnanians. The alliances which the three powers had concluded in 230 were, therefore, a dead letter.

Appian shows that the Greek and other states that had surrendered to the Romans were subjects of the Romans vis-à-vis the world at large, and his testimony is confirmed by Polybius.[82] The states concerned had surrendered themselves unconditionally for the most part; that is to say, they had performed *deditio*.[83] *Deditio* legally placed those who had performed the act *(dediticii)* in the same status as those whose cities had been taken by storm.[84] Although theoretically the *dediticius* was at the absolute disposal of the Roman state, a power which had placed itself voluntarily in this status could expect relatively lenient treatment[85] and could be placed in virtually any of the legal categories in which the Roman government viewed other societies.[86] Accordingly a grant of *libertas* to the state concerned could follow *deditio*. Even if it be correct to regard a grant of *libertas* as canceling *deditio* and therefore being an absolute and not a precarious grant, in practice any state weak enough to place itself under Roman protection must follow Roman wishes. Such states, moreover, became "friends" of Rome *(amici populi Romani)*, and as such were regularly expected to follow Roman leadership in foreign affairs.[87] We know that Apollonia and Corcyra were set "free" by the Romans.[88] In all probability the other states that "surrendered themselves unto the Roman faith" were also proclaimed "free." But since these states were also viewed as Roman subjects, it is clear that their *libertas* turned out to be the limited *libertas* of independence in local affairs. To use Holleaux's term,[89] the Romans established a "protectorate" in Illyria and some near-by places. That the Greeks concerned, however, understood these fine distinctions of Roman technique in foreign affairs is extremely doubtful.[90] They had the greater reason to misunderstand since the Roman yoke was so light. They paid no taxes to Rome, nor were their territories occupied by Roman officials or troops.[91] In the winter of 229/8 the consul Postumius,[92] wintering at Epidamnus, levied troops from the surrounding cities. But the contribution of occasional troops for wars, especially for one like this in their own defense, could not be considered a heavy burden; nor could the obligation to follow the Romans in foreign affairs be so considered. These were all second- or third-rate powers, accustomed to being satellites in the orbit of some great power throughout most of their history.

All this the Acarnanians and Epirotes could ponder in the years after the First Illyrian War. By this time Rome had brought most of the western Greeks under her sway. The Epirotes and the Acarnanians could now observe the results close at hand. Particularly the governing classes, the oligarchs, in both states could observe with interest the Roman protection of the propertied elements in society.[93] The same ruling classes could also consider that Rome had easily defeated the Illyrians who had shortly before been the terror of western Greece and who had disgracefully routed both the Achaeans and the Aetolians.

The Epirotes in particular might give thought to these matters. Not only was Corcyra, just across the strait, in Roman hands, but so was the former Epirote territory of Atintania, which formed a narrow salient projecting far into Epirus and controlling the passes leading into the interior of the country. Phoenice itself, the capital of Epirus, was only a few miles from Atintania. The district now, presumably, had local independence.

The Epirotes, like the Acarnanians former allies of the Illyrians, were in no position to expect favors from the Romans. Had the Epirotes wanted such favors, in all likelihood they should have imitated the example of Demetrius of Pharos and gone over to the Roman side. Atintania, therefore, was not given back to Epirus. It might be argued that Roman control of Atintania was partly a precaution against any resuscitation of the Epirote-Illyrian alliance.[94]

In any event, to our knowledge no embassy was sent either to Epirus or to Acarnania. Postumius had sent embassies to the Achaean and Aetolian Leagues to explain Roman purposes and accomplishments in the late war (228 B.C.), and shortly thereafter envoys were sent by the senate to Athens and Corinth.[95] The omission of embassies to Epirus and Acarnania, the allies of the Illyrian enemies of Rome and the neighbors of the new "protectorate," therefore seems deliberate. Accordingly, in 229/8 not even *amicitia* of the most informal variety came into existence between the Romans and the Acarnanians or the Epirotes. The first stage of Roman policy toward Acarnania and Epirus was one of completely ignoring the very existence of the latter powers officially.

It seems to me that this fact affords some support to the theory of Holleaux that the Romans had no interest in eastern imperialism at this time. If they had had such an interest, it would have cost them nothing to send an embassy to Acarnania and Epirus. Such an embassy could have cautioned the two powers to avoid disreputable allies in the future, and the Epirote and Acarnanian governments could have given as an official answer what the Romans must certainly have known already: that they had not entered the Illyrian alliance as free agents. Such an embassy would have cleared the atmosphere and given the Romans something to build on in the future. Evidently, outside of the necessary job of policing the lower Adriatic, they were as yet at pains to make no commitments of any kind whatsoever in the east.

Chapter II

THE FIRST MACEDONIAN WAR: FROM INDIFFERENCE TO *AMICITIA*

ROME COULD WITH IMPUNITY disregard the Epirotes and the Acarnanians in her settlement of Adriatic affairs in 228. If a new Pyrrhus or Alexander the Molossian was to arise in the Greek world, there were no indications that he would be found again in Epirus. The entire history of Epirus since the death of Pyrrhus I in 272 had been one of almost continuous decline in prestige and progressive loss of territory. It required no particular degree of diplomatic astuteness to discover this; it must have been a fact patent to all. On the other hand, the same could not be said of Macedonia. True, the fortunes of the Macedonians in 229 were at perhaps a lower ebb than in the entire half-century preceding. Besides, the nominal ruler of Macedonia in 229 was Philip V, a child — although the government had been entrusted to Antigonus Doson, who was shortly to demonstrate his great abilities and to become king in his own right. Nevertheless in 229 there was no guarantee that Macedonia would remain in a condition of humiliating impotence indefinitely. Macedonia must resent the establishment of a Roman "protectorate" so close to her western borders.[1] It is very unfortunate that our scanty sources give us no information on the important subject of Macedonian reaction to the "protectorate"; our reasoning must in the last analysis pretty largely depend upon *a priori* grounds. In effect, would any great power view with indifference the establishment of the influence of another great power in an area contiguous to the territory of the first power? Unless one is prepared to argue that not only the forms and expressions of ancient statecraft, but even the basic principles of its operation, differed radically from our own, the answer must be that Macedonia could not fail to view with anxiety the establishment of Roman hegemony in the lands just across the mountains to the west. Moreover, this "protectorate" included, as Maurice Holleaux[2] has pointed out, the mouths of the Genusus, the Apsus, and the Aous, which were the western terminals of the routes into Macedonia. Rome also now controlled Atintania, the entrance not only to Epirus, but to Thessaly and Macedonia. Furthermore one cannot maintain that Macedonia had not been interested in the lands to the west. Beginning as early as the later fifth century B.C.,[3] the kings of Macedonia had interfered in these western lands whenever opportunity offered and Macedonia was sufficiently powerful.[4] As recently as during the preceding reign, the Macedonians had interfered in Epirus — as we have seen.[5] Since, therefore, Macedonian interests must have been adversely affected by the establishment of the "protectorate" in the west, it was almost inevitable that the Macedonian government would try to rid itself of that "protectorate" as soon as two conditions were fulfilled: as soon as Macedonia had recovered her strength and position in the Balkan peninsula and the Aegean at home, and whenever thereafter the Romans might be sufficiently involved in the western Mediterranean to be unable to concentrate their entire strength in the east.

On the Roman side there is no reason to believe that there was any desire at this time for further penetration in the Balkans. The Roman embassies to the Greeks in 228 seem to have been only a diplomatic courtesy. On the other hand, it is quite probable that the Romans were aware that Macedonia was the ally of the Illyrians. It has been suggested that the large size of the armament which the Romans sent against Teuta was intended in part to deter or cope with any possible Macedonian aid to the Illyrians.[6] This may be so; on the other hand, other reasons might be suggested. Rome may have desired, for example, by her display of overwhelming force to overawe the Illyrians in the future into abiding by such settlement as she intended to impose. Whatever Roman intentions may have been, at any rate the size of the military and naval forces dispatched on this occasion may have served to make the Macedonian government realize that even a recovered Macedonia ought not to attack the Romans until the latter were well occupied elsewhere. There is also the fact that no embassy was dispatched either by the senate or by Postumius to Pella.[7] Gaetano de Sanctis[8] has perhaps interpreted this omission best. According to him, the Romans had simply established themselves in the Balkans for their own purposes and had acted as though no other power existed. In effect they had placed Macedonia in the same category as Epirus and Acarnania; insult had been added to injury.[9]

For the next decade the Romans left the Greeks entirely to themselves. During that period the political situation of Greece altered considerably. The ability of Antigonus Doson restored Macedonia to a position of dominance in the peninsula such as she had not known since the last years of Gonatas. For our present purpose it is most important to note that Epirus and Acarnania were once again drawn firmly into the Macedonian orbit. Such a development was clearly inherent in the logic of the situation. Second-rate powers such as Epirus and Acarnania must necessarily attach themselves to a stronger power in order to have any degree of security. The Illyrians were no longer available for such a purpose, and the Aetolians had by no means renounced their ambitions to acquire additional territory for their league in the west. The Achaeans as well as the Aetolians could scarcely have been well-disposed to Epirus and Acarnania after the former had abandoned them so unceremoniously in 230 and after the latter had fought against them in 229. Rome had left the two northwestern Greek states severely alone, and there was no reason to believe that she had reversed her determination to remain aloof. This left only Macedonia. For Acarnania a rapprochement with Macedonia offered no difficulties. Her appeal for aid to Demetrius II, or at least the appeal of the city of Medion, had prompted Illyrian intervention in the first place. For Epirus the situation was different. The Epirotes still bore the guilt of the overthrow of their kings, closely allied with Macedonia. But grudges are not long nursed in practical politics when it is expedient to forget them.[10] In the winter of 224/3 B.C., with Doson and the Achaeans (especially Achaea's great statesman Aratus?) as its mainsprings, a new panhellenic league was formed, including the Achaeans, Epirotes, Phocians, Macedonians, Boeotians, Acarnanians, Thessalians,[11] and the (Opuntian?) Locrians.[12] Our sources on the league's foundation are provokingly brief and vague.[13] Nevertheless it seems likely that the adherence of the Epirotes and Acarnanians must have come about through Antigonus. A friendly understanding must have existed between the Epirotes and the Acarnanians on the one hand and the power that brought them into the league on the other, before the entrance of the two northwestern powers into the league. This was probably Antigonus; for the Achaeans, who had repeatedly failed miserably against Cleomenes of Sparta, were in no position to offer protection to Epirus and Acarnania, even if the Achaeans were willing to overlook their grievances of 230/29. It is impossible to say exactly when the various powers concerned entered the league. It was certainly before Sellasia (222, or at latest 221) that Epirus and Acarnania joined, for they contributed troops to the side of the allies at that battle.[14] It is very unlikely that Epirus and Acarnania would remain in "splendid isolation" long after 228; it was too dangerous. It seems fairly probable then that they joined the Hellenic League quite early, perhaps as early as the spring of 223, and that they had reached some sort of understanding with Antigonus, who probably brought them into the league, some years before that.[15]

The new Hellenic League, thus joined by the Epirotes and the Acarnanians, was a fairly loose one, although the league covenants seem to have provided that no state could take any action contrary to the league agreements.[16] Among other things this must mean that secession was forbidden. By virtue of his office the king of Macedonia was head of the league (*hegemon*) and commander of its armed forces in event of war as well. The league possessed a *synedrion* or council which was convoked at various times by the *hegemon*. Declaration of war by the *synedrion* had to be approved by the individual members. Since secession from the league was forbidden, it follows that a state which did not ratify a declaration of war must have been bound to remain neutral.[17] While league members were bound to enter into no diplomatic relations with any other king,[18] the *hegemon* might not interfere in the internal concerns of the allies.[19] The original purpose of the league was to deal with Cleomenes of Sparta and the social revolution which he represented.[20] Obviously the Epirote and Acarnanian governments would be not at all unwilling to join a society for the preservation of the status quo. But the provision of the original agreements against secession and probably the long duration of the league as well[21] indicate that it was designed to be an organization with indefinite life. If so, and if one believes that Doson was seriously perturbed by the Roman "protectorate," it is hard to avoid the suspicion that he may very well have had the Romans in the back of his mind when he formed the league. Yet it would be easy to exaggerate this element in the formation of the league.[22] Such a purpose obviously could not have been openly avowed in the league covenants. To have stated such a purpose would have irretrievably compromised Antigonus and Aratus (assuming that the latter would have acquiesced in such a program — a large assumption) before they were ready. Even to have discussed such matters secretly among the allies would probably have been detrimental to the league. The Greek states were quite willing to go along with operations against Cleomenes and social change; yet it is reasonable to suspect that they might well have balked at any program that included an eventual attack on the great power which a few years before had made short work of a people who had terrorized Greece without punishment. If Antigonus had any such ideas, he kept them to himself. But the king of Macedonia was an able and sober statesman. In the light of the entire history of Greece for more than a century past, he might well have grave doubts that a league of Greek states would long support Macedonia in determined opposition to another great power. The rule forbidding diplomatic negotiations with another king shows how little Antigonus trusted his Greek allies.[23] If Antigonus had Rome in mind when he founded the Hellenic League, he might have reasoned that in degree varying according to circumstances it might be of some use to Macedonia in a struggle with Rome.

Furthermore, it is extremely unlikely that Epirus and Acarnania went into the league with any particular anti-Roman intention in mind. What they wanted was security in both domestic and foreign affairs. The league promised to procure both kinds of peace. On the other hand the two northwestern Greek powers were now definitely in the Macedonian sphere of influence, and in the future any power opposed to Macedonia must take them into its calculations as potentially hostile to itself, *prima facie* at least.

Epirus and Acarnania were not the only powers on the west coast of Greece to assist Doson and the allies at Sellasia. Demetrius of Pharos, who owed his principality to Rome,[24] brought a contingent of Illyrians to fight Cleomenes.[25] This alliance manifestly could not have been formed at the time of the battle; it probably was some years old at that time. Since Demetrius began to break away from allegiance to Rome at the time of the Gallic War (beginning in

225 B.C.), the rapprochement with Doson is usually dated to about 225 B.C.[26] Emboldened by the alliance with Macedonia, Demetrius not only sailed with fifty *lemboi* beyond Lissus, contrary to the treaty of 228, to engage in piracy as far away as the southern Aegean, but proceeded to sack and destroy places in the Roman "protectorate," places "subject to Rome" (221/20 B.C.).[27] Appian adds[28] that Demetrius detached Atintania from the "protectorate." There is no reason to believe that this means anything more than that Demetrius' operations against the "protectorate" included Atintania.[29] In 220 on another piratical foray, which also extended around Greece into the Aegean, Demetrius was accompanied by his fellow Illyrian princeling, Scerdilaidas.[30] Rome was now free of the Gallic War, but the Second Punic War threatened to break out at any time. The Roman government determined to protect itself in the East during the coming conflict by disposing of Demetrius. A brief campaign in the summer of 219 sufficed to expel the Illyrian from his principality. Demetrius fled to the court of Philip V, the new king of Macedonia, and being hospitably received, spent the rest of his life in the service of the Macedonian monarch.[31] It is noteworthy that Demetrius found it necessary, just before the Roman forces appeared, to put opponents of his policy in the "protectorate" to death.[32] Either a considerable number of persons in the few years since 228 had come to favor the Roman "protectorate," or at least they recognized the futility of resistance to Rome.

What has seemed strange is that Demetrius himself did not see the futility of his defiance of the Romans. Inasmuch as Demetrius was the ally of Macedonia in which, Polybius[33] says, he placed all his hopes, it has been suggested that Demetrius had been egged on by Philip.[34] Another passage in Polybius[35] has been the basis of a suggestion[36] that in 220 Philip was in Epirus and that perhaps this visit was connected with Demetrius' exploits in that year. It has been answered[37] that it would have been madness for Macedonia, barely recovered under Doson, to bid defiance to Rome when the latter was still uninvolved elsewhere. Moreover, in 220 the cautious councilors of Doson were still in the ascendancy at Philip's court.[38] Besides, in his raid of 220 Demetrius with Scerdilaidas also attacked Pylos, although the place belonged to Philip's ally, the Achaean League. As for Philip's presence in

Epirus, the Greek is far from meaning necessarily that he was there; and even if Philip were there, his visit might well have been made for other reasons. Epirus was the land of Philip's mother, and in the Social War, then about to begin, it was necessary to secure the loyalty of the Adriatic neighbors of Aetolia.

The action of Demetrius is probably to be credited only to his own insouciant rashness. At the end of the third century the Illyrians were still at least semibarbarians possessing that characteristic irresponsibility with which Rome was to cope so many times in her dealings with barbarian tribes. The fickleness of Demetrius was to be matched in the next few years by that of Scerdilaidas, who switched from the Aetolians, to Philip, to the Romans with equal readiness. On the other hand, the fear of the Romans that behind Demetrius stood Macedonia[39] is quite understandable. The Italian (or Italiote Greek) traders in the east, if no one else, must surely have brought to Rome the news of Demetrius' rapprochement with Macedonia. If possible, the Romans must quell Demetrius before the Second Punic War broke out; for all the Roman government knew, the accord with Demetrius might well have been preliminary to an attack on themselves.[40] Indeed, they were probably right in the long view. Doson and Philip would not have struck at this juncture, but in the late 220's they might well look forward to a more propitious day when Demetrius' *lemboi* and his ports on the Adriatic would serve their purpose well. Demetrius' precipitancy spoiled their plans. Yet, even expelled from his principality, he might be useful in the future, for he must have had a party attached to his interests in his dominions. It seems possible that this consideration, as well as his past services to Doson, explains the welcome which Philip gave him in 219.[41]

As far as we know, the status of the Illyrian "protectorate" was little changed by the Second Illyrian War. Those states won over or seized by Demetrius resumed their status of 228.[42] Nor did the Romans enter into any diplomatic relations with any Greek state. Granted that the Romans had not changed their ideas about further interference in Greece since 228 (and there is absolutely no reason to suppose that they had, especially in view of the war in the west about to begin), it is quite understandable that Rome paid no attention to the Greeks. The action taken by the Roman government was probably viewed by it as exclusively its own concern. It had simply put down a rebellion in its own dominions; this did not have to be explained to anybody.

The policy of the Romans in Greece as a whole remained unchanged; this is also true with reference to Epirus and Acarnania. The two powers to the south of Demetrius' principality were ignored as before. But if any Roman statesman had given them any thought, he might well have arrived at the conclusion that the two powers could be classed as potential enemies at least. In 229 the Epirotes and Acarnanians had been the allies of the Illyrian pirates whom Rome had fought; in 219 the two states were the allies of a reinvigorated Macedonia, which the Romans suspected of intriguing with Demetrius against the "protectorate." The geographical situation of the two Greek states rendered them capable of the same nuisance value as Demetrius of Pharos. Yet neither they nor Macedonia had made any overt move. The Romans, having achieved their immediate objective of ridding themselves of Demetrius, could turn to more pressing affairs in the west. This they could do the more readily since for the present Macedonia and her allies were fully engaged with other concerns — the Social War.[43]

Antigonus Doson had died in the summer of 221 B.C. and had been succeeded on the throne of Macedonia by Philip V, still little more than a boy.[44] Almost at once the Aetolians seized the occasion to put the untried youthful monarch to the test[45] by harassing various members of the Hellenic League. In addition to raids conducted in the Peloponnese and elsewhere, the Aetolians ravaged the coast of Epirus and tried to seize the Acarnanian city of Thyrrheum (autumn, 221 B.C.).[46] The next year the Aetolians resumed operations in the Peloponnese. Among other counter measures the Achaeans sent embassies to Philip and the allies asking that the league bring aid, and that Messene, which was also endangered by the aggressions of the Aetolians, be admitted to the league.[47] The previous expeditions of the Aetolians had not technically been official enterprises of the government; the Aetolian assembly now met and voted for peace with all concerned, including the Achaeans if the latter deserted the Messenians. Obviously this was a move to localize the conflict. The Aetolians had no stomach for a war against the entire Hellenic League, including Macedonia.[48] The allies presumably answered the Achaean request for aid as did the Epirotes and Philip. Messenian admission to the league was agreed to, but Philip and the allies refused to go to war with Aetolia.[49] It is possible that Philip was in Epirus at the time he and the Epirotes made this reply.[50] If so, it is unlikely that his visit there had anything to do with Demetrius of Pharos or Rome. One might suggest that he had come to reassure himself of the loyalty of the western Greeks to the league.[51] It is possible also that the king had made his visit to inspect what damage the Aetolians had done and to dissuade the western Greeks from undertaking any rash action against Aetolia. At any rate, the answer given the Achaeans by the Epirotes and the other allies was probably made in accordance with Philip's wishes.[52] At least if she were attacked by Aetolia, the adherence of Epirus to the league was doubtful, as the event proved. Presumably Philip could also recall the Epirote *volte-face* from the Achaean-Aetolian alliance to the Illyrian in 230.

If Philip had hoped that the Aetolians would come to their senses and back down before the prospect of a general Hellenic war, he was mistaken. The Aetolians may have interpreted the refusal of Philip and the allies to aid Achaea as a sign of weakness. Soon after the temporizing reply of the allies to the Achaean government, the Aetolian Agelaus and Demetrius of Pharos conducted a joint raid into Achaean territory. Demetrius' colleague, Scerdilaidas, also allied himself with the Aetolians.[53] Once again Aratus, the Achaean *strategos,* appealed to Philip for assistance.[54] In the summer of 220 B.C. the *synedrion* of the Hellenic League met at Corinth. Along with many other accusations of Aetolian wrongdoing brought by the allies, the Acarnanians and Epirotes complained of the Aetolian raids on Epirus and the attempt on Thyrrheum.[55] The *synedrion* of the league unanimously voted for war with Aetolia. To the declaration of war various pledges were added. It was agreed that the allies would recover all lands and cities seized by the Aetolians since the death of Demetrius II (229 B.C.), also that any who had been compelled to join the Aetolian League against their will "by force of circumstances" should be freed and made sovereign once again.[56] As far as Epirus was concerned, this latter clause would probably include Ambracia and Amphilochia,[57] while the Acarnanians would recover the territory lost to the Aetolians at the time of the partition in the days of Alexander II of Epirus.[58] Therefore Epirus and Acarnania had much to gain by a successful war against Aetolia.

The constitution of the Hellenic League required that declarations of war be ratified by the individual members, and the Acarnanians promptly confirmed the resolution of the *synedrion*.[59] The Epirotes, however, confirmed the decree with the proviso that they would make war as soon as Philip himself took the field. Nevertheless an Aetolian embassy was informed by the Epirote government that Epirus had resolved to remain at peace with Aetolia.[60] Evidently if Philip did visit Epirus some months before, he was well-advised in doing so. Epirote foreign policy in this whole period beginning with 230 B.C. is very "realistic," to put the kindest interpretation on it. The only explanation must be that the Epirotes were extremely fearful of the Aetolians, and that they were by no means certain that Philip would or could pull their own particular chestnuts out of the fire in the ensuing war. One can only conclude that Epirus would have remained strictly neutral, had Philip not appeared in the west the next year. The presence of an Aetolian embassy in Epirus suggests that the Aetolians hoped either to procure Epirote neutrality or perhaps even to detach the Epirotes from the league altogether.[61] That the Aetolians had this hope in turn suggests that Aetolia was not without friends in Epirus.

Although it would be rash to assert that Philip yet had any definite plans for an attack upon the Roman "protectorate" in Illyria, nevertheless Philip's campaigns in the west during the Social War must mean that he desired to strengthen his hold upon the loyalty of Epirus and Acarnania. Whatever other reasons may have led him to gratify the two western powers, it is hard to avoid the conclusion that he was keeping his fences there well mended with a possible view to future operations against the Romans.[62]

In the summer of 219 Philip passed through Thessaly and arrived in Epirus. Joined by the entire Epirote levy, he marched through Epirus to the Ambraciote plain in the south. Here the city of Ambracia, the reconquest of which for Epirus was part of the announced program of the allies, was protected by an important fortress called Ambracus. Although the Aetolians had invaded Philip's own dominions, he sat down before Ambracus and took the place within forty days. The fortress was handed over to the

Epirotes and Philip continued on his way south.[63] Passing across the Ambracian Gulf into Acarnania, Philip was joined in the latter country by two thousand Acarnanian foot and two hundred horse. There followed a campaign against Aetolia in which Philip entered that part of Acarnania which was subject to Aetolia. The principal Acarnanian cities here were Phoetiae, Stratus, Metropolis, and Oeniadae.[64] The king took Phoetiae,[65] and Oeniadae, the latter of which he strongly fortified as a port of embarkation for the Peloponnese.[66] In accordance with the pledges made at Corinth in 220 these cities were turned over to the Acarnanians. In addition the king took and burned Metropolis, although the Aetolians retained the citadel.[67] Likewise the territory of Stratus had been ravaged, the Aetolians not daring to offer any resistance.[68] From Oeniadae, however, Philip was recalled to Macedonia by the news of an intended raid in force being prepared by the Dardanian barbarians to the north.[69] Philip's main objective in this campaign, "the systematic opening up of a western coast route [to the Peloponnese] through the friendly territories of Epirus, western Ambracia, and Acarnania" had been achieved.[70] He had also been in a position to observe the Romans operating against Demetrius in Illyria that summer, a matter obviously of interest to him.[71] How far had he conciliated the good will of the Epirotes and the Acarnanians? Probably the latter were fairly well satisfied with the acquisition of two important cities, although it is quite likely that they wanted Stratus and Metropolis as well. The Epirotes, however, may have been quite disgruntled at not being able to acquire Ambracia itself.[72] The possession of Ambracus without Ambracia was presumably of comparatively little value. Hence the Epirotes might reflect that in 219 their alliance with Philip had profited them little more than their neutrality would have, while at the same time they had committed themselves to the war. When in the autumn of the same year (219) Dorimachus, the new Aetolian *strategos*, ravaged the southeastern sections of Epirus and even laid waste the sacred structures of Dodona with fire, the Epirotes had even more cause to rue their decision to side openly with Philip.[73]

During the winter Philip conducted his famous surprise campaign against his enemies in the Peloponnese. For the campaigning season of 218, however, the king determined to continue the war with a vigorous naval offensive.[74] In the spring of 218 Philip wrote to the Messenians, Epirotes, Acarnanians, and Scerdilaidas to join him at Cephallenia, and sailed from Patrae, bound for the island.[75] An attack on Cephallenia, allied with the Aetolians, was an important thrust against Aetolian naval power. Such an attack was also bound to enlist the sympathies of the northwest Greeks, for the Cephallenians had helped the Aetolians in the raid on the coast of Epirus in 221,[76] and the Aetolians seem to have made such raids on the coast of Epirus and Acarnania a habit.[77] Although the contingents from Epirus, Acarnania, and the others arrived at Cephallenia, the allies were unable to take the city of Pale to which they laid siege.[78] Meanwhile the Aetolians had invaded Thessaly while their Spartan allies had attacked Messenia. Envoys from Messenia urged Philip to sail across to the Peloponnese; other envoys from Acarnania urged the king to force the withdrawal of the Aetolians from Thessaly by an attack upon Aetolia. The natural base for such an attack would, of course, be Acarnania, and the latter country might reasonably expect to profit therefrom. The Achaean statesman Aratus supported the recommendations of the Acarnanians; and when it was pointed out to Philip that he would be shut up in the Peloponnese for the summer by the Etesian winds, if he sailed thither, he decided to accept the Acarnanian alternative.[79] The king sailed to Limnaea, a place in Acarnania on the Ambracian Gulf. In Acarnania he was joined by the full Acarnanian levy under the command of the Acarnanian *strategos*, Aristophantus, but the Epirotes were unable to mobilize their forces in time, for Philip determined to act with utmost speed.[80] The Acarnanians and Philip's forces then marched rapidly into Aetolia, pillaged the countryside as they advanced, sacked the Aetolian sanctuary at Thermum, and as rapidly returned to Limnaea.[81] Thence Philip sailed to Corinth,[82] and the campaigning for that year in northwest Greece was over. The results for Epirus and Acarnania were less than before. The Acarnanians had had a share of the rich booty of the Thermum campaign; on the other hand, the Epirotes did not even have this to balance the expense of the abortive attack on Pale.

Worse was to follow the next year. Scerdilaidas, resentful at not receiving the full subvention which Philip had promised him, sent out fifteen ships which treacherously took four of Philip's ships in the harbor of Leucas. Thereafter the Illyrian squadron sailed south to Malea, bent on piracy.[83] In the same year (217) Agetas, the Aetolian *strategos,* with the Aetolian levy en masse descended upon Epirus and Acarnania and pillaged them with impunity. An Acarnanian counterattack on Stratus failed through a sudden panic.[84]

The war, however, was about to end suddenly. Certainly the Epirotes, if not the Acarnanians as well, would welcome its termination. While Philip was attending the Nemean games at Argos, a messenger brought him the news of Hannibal's great victory over the Roman consul C. Flaminius at Lake Trasimenus in Etruria. Philip showed the letter at first only to Demetrius of Pharos, who advised him to end the Social War at once and seize the opportunity to rid himself of the Roman "protectorate."[85] Philip followed this advice and almost at once opened peace negotiations with the Aetolians.[86] Polybius[87] represents Demetrius as arousing Philip's ambition by suggesting that an expedition to Italy should follow the reduction of the Illyrian "protectorate," and that such an expedition in turn would be the first step toward the conquest of the world. It is by no means impossible that Demetrius made such statements.[88] It would be fairly well in keeping with his impulsive and irresponsible nature if he had. Philip was informed of the new development in the west by a courier with a letter from Macedonia. This in itself would seem to indicate that he had an interest in events in Italy. When Philip showed Demetrius the lettter he swore him to silence. The implication is that Philip regarded the matter as an important affair of state before Demetrius made his recommendations. If so, it might very well signify that Philip had already been considering the possibility of interfering in the west if the course of the Punic War should offer a favorable opportunity.[89] Whatever may have been the new and splendid vistas of a larger arena for his ambition which the advice of Demetrius may have awakened in Philip,[90] the two conditions for an attempt on the Illyrian "protectorate" of Rome were now seemingly fulfilled: Macedonia had recovered from her weakness of 229/8 and Rome was fully occupied in the western Mediterranean.[91]

While peace negotiations were in progress, Philip sailed to Zacynthus, an important base for a western expedition, and brought the island under his control.[92] Peace was made at Naupactus on the basis of *uti possidetis*,[93] a far cry from the original objectives of the war.[94] In view of the pillaging their country had undergone at the hands of the Aetolians, the Epirotes were probably quite relieved at the restoration of peace, despite the fact that all they had obtained was Ambracus. On the other hand the Acarnanians had regained two of their lost cities and had probably profited considerably by the pillage of Thermum and Aetolia. At Naupactus the Epirote and Acarnanian delegates heard the Aetolian statesman Agelaus deliver his famous speech about the clouds looming in the west, and his warning that the victor in the Punic War would quite likely not be satisfied with rule over the Italiote and Siceliote Greeks, but would attempt to extend his sway over the Greek homeland as well.[95]

After the congress at Naupactus Philip had to hasten north to deal with Scerdilaidas, who had invaded Macedonian Pelagonia. Philip's campaign was a great success; Scerdilaidas was repelled and large sections of Illyria were added to the Macedonian dominions (autumn, 217).[96] These new acquisitions included most of the land (Dassaretia) between Lake Lychnus and the river Apsus. Thus Philip's territories now reached to the verge of the Roman "protectorate" and the frontier of northern Epirus.[97]

During the following winter, in order to be equipped to attack the "protectorate" by sea,[98] Philip constructed a hundred *lemboi*. Having also trained his crews for the purpose, he set sail in the spring of 216 for western Greek waters. While he was sailing past the coast of southern Illyria, he learned that some Roman quinqueremes had been sighted. In the erroneous belief that a major Roman armada was on its way, Philip turned back precipitately and accomplished nothing else that year. Actually the Roman fleet included only ten quinqueremes, which the Romans had dispatched in answer to a plea for help from Scerdilaidas.[99] Whatever the reason for this turning back — and certainly a hundred *lemboi* could not hope to withstand a large fleet of quinqueremes—Philip suffered considerable loss of prestige.[100] The Epirotes and Acarnanians might very well conclude that Philip was by no means equipped or prepared to withstand a large-scale naval attack upon the Adriatic coasts.

In 215 B.C. Philip finally entered upon an alliance with Hannibal. Polybius has preserved the actual terms of this treaty.[101]

In this document the principal provision in favor of Philip was that the Roman domination of Corcyra, Apollonia, Epidamnus, Pharos, Dimale, the Parthinians, and Atintania would cease;[102] in other words the Roman "protectorate" in Illyria was to be abolished.

The text of the treaty with Hannibal shows that the ambassadors sent to negotiate with Hannibal represented not only Philip but his allies as well.[103] Unfortunately the text of Polybius is fragmentary at this point and we have no notice whatever of action taken by the allies, who must of course be members of the Hellenic League. Whether or not the *synedrion* had met to authorize Philip to act in behalf of the allies cannot be determined. At least, however, Philip felt himself qualified to represent the allies in concluding this treaty. Yet such an act, involving the allies in a war with Rome, must be ratified by the members of the league severally. A league member which did not ratify a declaration of war was almost certainly expected to be neutral.[104] Of the two members of the league with whom we are concerned, there is no doubt that Acarnania ratified the decree of the *synedrion* and went to war with Rome, as the history of the First Macedonian War abundantly testifies.[105] The case of Epirus is not so clear.

On two occasions during the ensuing war Polybius lists the Epirotes as Philip's allies.[106] On the first occasion an Acarnanian ambassador, Lyciscus, is speaking at Sparta. His speech is *ex parte,* its object being to persuade the Spartans not to join the Aetolians and the Romans against the Hellenic League and Macedonia. One of the points the orator makes is that entering the war on the Aetolian side is to join with the barbarian against Epirotes, Achaeans, Acarnanians, Boeotians, and Thessalians — that is, "almost all the Greeks except the Aetolians." Obviously the speaker is trying to produce the belief on the part of his audience that it will be opposing virtually all Greece if it joins the Aetolian-Roman side. Therefore he may well have named the members of the league at random without paying strict attention to whether all the members so-named were actually at war with the Aetolians or not. The second time the Epirotes are listed as Philip's allies is on a similar occasion. This time an ambassador, whose identity is not preserved in the extant fragments of Polybius, is arguing that the Aetolians are actually fighting to bring about the enslavement of Greece. Philip's allies, against whom the Aetolians are fighting, are then listed—

and the Epirotes are included. These, then, are the Greeks whom the Aetolians are actually trying to enslave, and it is obviously to the advantage of the orator to make the list as long and impressive as possible.

Some other facts also bear upon the problem. The Epirotes were instrumental in bringing about peace at the end of the war, out of their "taedio diuturni belli."[107] Such an expression might imply that the Epirotes were neutral in the war, or it might imply that they were weary of a war in which they had participated. But neutrals, especially those situated right in the middle of one of the theaters of operations, could well be tired of a war, or find it irksome, or a nuisance. Again, when the Acarnanians wished to remove their noncombatants to a safe place, as they did in 211, they sent them to Epirus.[108] Besides, the sources would seem to record no military activity against Epirus in the war.[109] Finally, it has been shown above how the Epirotes attempted to preserve a *de facto* neutrality in the Social War; and how, when they were induced to enter that war in the hope of territorial gains when Philip appeared in the west in 219, they gained little and lost much thereafter. In addition Philip's naval fiasco of 216 must have shown the Epirotes that the king could not protect them from Roman inroads by sea. It seems very probable, accordingly, that the Epirotes preserved a status of *de facto* neutrality in the First Macedonian War.[110] Both the Romans and Philip derived advantage from Epirote neutrality. For the Romans it meant one less enemy; for Philip one less ally in Greece to protect (especially after 211).

This leaves the question of the legal status of the neutrality unsettled. It has been suggested[111] that when the Romans concluded a treaty of alliance with Aetolia against Philip in 211 they deliberately omitted any mention of hostilities against a country so near their "protectorate" as Epirus. But while our knowledge of that treaty probably is incomplete, the treaty did specify that in the direction of the "protectorate" the Aetolians were to be allowed to acquire territory only as far as Corcyra.[112] This would include a large part of southern Epirus, even if one takes "Corcyra" to mean the southern tip of that island; nor could there be any mistake on the part of anyone who had sailed along the Epirote coast. Another possibility is that the Romans may have come to an understanding with the Epirote government, or a party in Epirus that favored Rome, to the effect that the Epirotes would not be disturbed if they did not participate in the war. At any rate, in 205 Philip listed the Epirotes on his side in the peace treaty.[113] This probably means that the Epirotes had legally been at war with Rome. Hence the two orators who, according to Polybius, listed Epirus as an ally of Philip in this war were technically right, but still exaggerating. That a private, and more or less treacherous, accord with the Romans is conceivable is shown by the parallel Epirote answer to the Aetolians in 220.[114] If there was a pro-Aetolian party in Epirus at that time, this same party might well be pro-Roman, at least after 211 when Rome and Aetolia became allies. We need postulate no attachment to either power necessarily—only fear. Finally, there is some reason to believe that if there was an informal understanding between Rome and Epirus, contrary to the Epirotes' obligations to the Hellenic League, it was probably entered into after the Roman-Aetolian treaty of 211 had been concluded.[115] It was not until then that the Romans began to pursue a really active policy in Greece. The fact that the Roman-Aetolian treaty of that year seems to view Epirus, or part of it, as a potential acquisition for the Aetolians also suggests that the understanding with Epirus was later than the treaty with Aetolia.

Even after Philip's alliance with Hannibal in 215 the Romans limited themselves to a minimum effort in Greece. This lack of enterprise may well reflect their distaste for further involvement in the Balkans,[116] but the primary reason must have been that they did not fear Philip's intervention in Italy and did not wish further to disperse their forces unnecessarily. How was Philip to get to Italy with a Roman guard force of fifty ships under M. Valerius Laevinus[117] patrolling the lower Adriatic coasts of the peninsula; and once there, what would the king use for a port of debarkation? The safety of the "protectorate" could well be sacrificed temporarily to the security of Italy.

Obviously Philip's first objective must be the "protectorate"—both for its own sake, and because, if he ever intended to attempt to bring the war to Italy, it would if unreduced constitute a grave menace to his lines of communications with Macedonia. The ports of the "protectorate" would also be a convenient jumping-off point for any Italian venture. In late summer of 214 Philip commenced his attack by sea. The inhabitants of Oricus, an Illyrian town in the "protectorate," appealed for aid to Laevinus, whose instructions included an injunction "to keep watch over the Macedonian War."[118] Laevinus sailed at once to Illyria, where he trapped the king between hostile Illyrian tribes and the sea. Philip was compelled to burn his ships and beat an inglorious retreat over the mountains to his own country.[119] Thus the lesson read to the western Greek powers in 216 was repeated.[120] Moreover, the incident shows that Apollonia, at least, and probably most of the Greek cities of the "protectorate," had no desire to leave the protection of Rome, for Philip had tried to persuade the Apollonians to revolt from Rome. Yet the latter had preferred to risk the dangers of a siege rather than go over to Philip.[121]

We have no connected narrative for the next two years, but it emerges from scattered references in Polybius and Livy that Philip occupied himself in cutting away the hinterland of the "protectorate," including the strategic Atintania, and finally penetrated to the Adriatic at Lissus. Obviously the Romans were confining their efforts to a minimum, trying to hold only the coast, the most vital part of their sphere of influence, the door to Italy.[122]

With the acquistion of a port of embarkation on the Adriatic, and with Tarentum for debarkation in Italy shortly to fall to his ally Hannibal (in 212, or possibly 213),[123] Philip might venture a crossing to Italy. Whether or not Philip actually would have made such an attempt at this time,[124] Rome could not run the risk. Hence in 212 B.C. Laevinus bestirred himself to obtain further means of keeping Philip occupied in Greece.[125] The Aetolians had lost much by the treaty of Naupactus in 217, and the cessation of hostilities cut them off from one of their chief sources of revenue—booty. Hence they had rapidly become discontented with the peace settlement. Besides, the Aetolians were already the friends or allies of a number of powers actually or potentially the enemies of Macedonia: Messenia, Elis, Sparta, and Attalus, the king of Pergamum.[126] Accordingly Laevinus initiated guarded discussions with the leading statesmen of Aetolia with a view to forming an alliance against Philip.[127] Having thus laid the groundwork, in 211 Laevinus addressed the Aetolian assembly. Along with other arguments the Roman admiral held out to the assembly the hope of regaining the Acarnanians who had been lost to them—presumably in the Social War. Livy goes on to say that the hope of gaining control of Acarnania was Laevinus' most effective argument.[128] There is some contradiction here,[129] but it is perhaps more apparent than real. We may suppose that Laevinus first promised the Aetolians those parts of Acarnania which they had once held, but lost in the Social War; then the success of this promise may have led him later on to promise them all Acarnania. The treaty actually concluded implied, as far as we know, that the Aetolians would be permitted to annex all of Acarnania if it were conquered, and a specific clause was added to the effect that the Romans would give help in executing the project.

Laevinus succeeded in his purpose; the Aetolians concluded a treaty with him which was ratified at Rome two years later. Among other things the treaty provided that various friends or allies of either state might be included later. The Aetolians were to make war on Philip by land, the Romans assisting at sea with at least twenty-five quinqueremes. Movable booty should become the property of the Romans, but conquered territory and cities should belong to the Aetolians, except that Aetolian acquisitions in the direction of the "protectorate" should not include any territory beyond Corcyra. Neither the Aetolians nor the Romans should make a separate peace with Philip.[130] Thus Acarnania was used as an attractive bait for the Aetolians. There is nothing surprising in this, or in the fact that southern Epirus was also potentially surrendered to the Aetolians by the treaty. Rome had so far shown no sign of wishing to interfere further in Greece than she had. Accordingly she had no interest in the fate of these states.[131] On the other hand, both in 229 and 219 the two powers had been allies of foes of Rome, avowed or implicit. From a policy of ignoring Epirus and Acarnania, in 212/11 Rome changed to one of official or potential hostility. This policy was probably modified, however, as far as Epirus was concerned, by an informal understanding which allowed Epirus to preserve its neutrality.

The Acarnanians, however, began almost at once to feel the heavy hand of Roman hostility. The same summer (211) that the accord with Aetolia had been negotiated, Laevinus took the Acarnanian town of Oeniadae, together with another place called Nasos,[132] and delivered them over to the Aetolians in accordance with the treaty.[133] Later that same year, after the Acarnanians had lost Oeniadae—probably in the early autumn—the Aetolians prepared a descent on Acarnania in full force. The Acarnanians dispatched their women and children and men over sixty to Epirus, and prepared for resistance to the death. At the same time they sent Philip a desperate appeal for help. The Aetolians, already daunted by the frantic preparations of their intended victims, gave up the project on the news that Philip was hastening to the assistance of his allies.[134]

During the winter of 211/10 the Aetolians sent an ambassador to Lacedaemon to persuade the Spartans to make war on the league. The Acarnanian Lyciscus also appeared at Sparta to attempt to counteract the efforts of the Aetolians.[135] Lyciscus represents the Romans as barbarians attempting to enslave Greece; their alliance with the Aetolians is directed against all Greece; the way in which the Romans make war is unprincipled and inhuman.[136] The bitterness of the speech probably represents the attitude of most Acarnanians toward the Romans at this time, although some allowance must be made for rhetoric.

After 211, as far as we know, the scene of major activity in the war shifted farther east, and no major campaign involving Acarnania took place in northwest Greece. Nevertheless the Acarnanians were subject to Aetolian raids from time to time. In 208 they asked Philip for help in repelling these attacks, but although the assistance was promised there is no evidence that it was sent.[137] Evidently the Aetolians, characteristically, did not feel themselves bound by any informal accord their Roman allies might have reached with the Epirotes, for a delegation from the latter people waited on Philip at the same time as the Acarnanians, presumably with the same request.[138]

In the years 207/6 B.C. the Romans did virtually nothing in the east[139] — whether Hasdrubal's invasion of Italy,[140] or the defeat of the Carthaginian fleet in 208,[141] or the strain of war on Italy coupled with the lack of success in the east,[142] or the Roman recapture of Tarentum, were the cause. Attalus of Pergamum, who had aided the Romans and the Aetolians in the earlier stages of the war, had also withdrawn. Taking advantage of the lack of enterprise of the Aetolians' principal allies, Philip was able to press his remaining foes more and more severely. The Aetolians appealed to Rome in vain for assistance.[143] Finally they were compelled to make a separate peace with Philip, probably in the winter of 206/5.[144] Later the Romans chose to regard this conclusion of a separate peace as terminating their alliance with the Aetolians.[145] Unfortunately we have no account of the provisions of this treaty, but it is certain that the Aetolians kept Oeniadae and, presumably, Nasos.[146]

In the spring of 205 B.C. the Romans, having evidently determined to resume major operations in Greece, sent to Greece a new commander, P. Sempronius Tuditanus. With him he brought ten thousand infantry, one thousand cavalry, and thirty-five warships.[147] This force was far in excess of what the Romans were supposed to send to Greece in accordance with the treaty of 211. It has usually been suggested that the reason for the large size of this force was the feeling on the part of the Romans that with the defeat of Hasdrubal and the conquest of Spain—Hannibal being reduced to virtual impotence—now was the time to come to conclusions with Philip.[148] More recently it has been implied strongly[149] that this expedition may well mark the first overt act of Roman imperialism in the east. Presumably the Romans must have realized that Philip was probably in no wise desirous of continuing the war; they must also have been aware that the king knew the cause of Hannibal and Carthage was already lost and the end was probably only a matter of time. Nevertheless the Romans dispatched this large expedition, an action which must mean that they intended a resumption of military activities in Greece on a larger scale than heretofore. Tuditanus, significantly, although not yet consul, was sent with proconsular authority.[150]

However that may be, it was impossible to continue the war in Greece without Aetolian assistance, unless the Romans were prepared to send a full-sized consular army to Greece. With the Punic War not yet over such an involvement in Greece was impractical, even had the senate been able to persuade the people of the advisability of such a step. And the Aetolians refused to break their recent peace with Philip.[151] On the other hand the revolt of the Parthini and neighboring tribes showed Philip that his hold on the interior of the "protectorate," conquered early in the war, was insecure.[152] Some desultory campaigning ensued; finally the Epirotes stepped into the breach.

The Epirotes, taking advantage of their informal neutrality in the conflict, and probably sufficiently canny to know that under the circumstances both the Romans and Philip were not averse to peace, first approached the Romans with the proposal that the Epirote government take steps to arrange a general peace (*pax communis*).[153] The Romans signified that they were agreeable, and the Epirotes thereupon approached Philip. The king agreed to a parley with the Roman commander at Phoenice, the Epirote capital. There, after a conference with the three *strategoi* of the Epirote *koinon*, Philip met Tuditanus. Other dignitaries were present at the conference: Epirote magistrates as well as King Amynander of Athamania and Acarnanian[154] representatives assisted. It is hard to explain the presence of Acarnanian delegates satisfactorily. It is very likely that this chapter of Livy is taken largely from Polybius[155] in a condensed version, but with Roman annalistic contaminations. Possibly representatives of all members of the Hellenic league which had participated in the war were there.[156] Possibly the mere propinquity of Acarnania is the answer, if the other members of the league were not there; but this seems very doubtful.

Philip, one (perhaps the senior) of the three Epirote *strategoi*, made a formal address urging both sides to conclude peace as a favor to the Epirotes.[157] Thereafter it was agreed by Tuditanus and King Philip that the Parthinians and other places in the "protectorate" should belong to the Romans, but that Atintania and probably most of Philip's conquests of 213 and 212 should be retained by the king.[158] The Romans were probably especially reluctant to lose Atintania because of its strategic position as the entrance to the south. In abortive peace negotiations in 209 one of the Roman demands, made through the Aetolians, had included the return of Atintania.[159] Again, in 205 according to Livy,[160] Philip was to have Atintania only if he sent a special embassy to Rome to procure the senate's consent. It looks as though Tuditanus may have been instructed that, if he had to make peace, he should try to keep Atintania, if at all possible. This eagerness to retain Atintania may well be an indication of senatorial desire to pursue a more active program in Greece, but it would be unwise to push this very far. On Philip's side the Epirotes and Acarnanians and other allies are mentioned as included in the treaty; the Romans also included various of their own "associates" (*socii*).[161]

Formally at least, this treaty marks a new epoch in the relations of Rome with Epirus and Acarnania. If "*amicitia* is the product of any non-hostile intercourse between Rome and a foreign state,"[162] then both Epirus and Acarnania, having technically been *hostes* of Rome before, now became *amici*. The language of the treaty as summarized by Livy[163] seems strongly to imply that Philip and Rome concluded the treaty and made it applicable to various of their "allies" or "associates."[164] *Amicitia* could exist without a *foedus*[165] and presumably there was not too much difference between the actual results of a *foedus amicitiae* and *amicitia sine foedere* in practice. Again, a treaty of peace could produce *amicitia* without being a *foedus amicitiae*. There seems no way of determining with certitude whether in Roman eyes Acarnania and Epirus became *amici* without *foedus*, or with *foedus* by virtue of this treaty; *i.e.*, did they in Roman eyes have a *foedus amicitiae* with Rome? The language of Livy seems to imply that they did not, that Rome recognized only Philip and herself as "high contracting powers" in the treaty,[166] but since they had both engaged in nonhostile relations with Rome (*i.e.*, the treaty), they must have become *amici*.[167]

During the late war the Epirotes had obviously been well treated by the Romans. Moreover, they had witnessed a war in which Rome had been able to handle the greatest power in the Balkans with little difficulty, even though most Roman resources were involved elsewhere. The Epirotes had also had, both in Illyria and Acarnania, an ample demonstration of how vulnerable the Adriatic states were to Roman attack from the sea. Their policy of neutrality alone had preserved them, presumably, from similar attacks. Such a policy would be useful if similar circumstances should ever recur. Presumably also they had conciliated some degree of Roman good will by helping negotiate the peace. All this does not mean, however, that they regarded the Romans with anything like affection, or that they did not regard them as barbarians who had interfered in Greece. But the Epirotes had reason, out of fear, to remain clear of an anti-Roman policy. Undoubtedly there must have been a faction which viewed such a policy as pusillanimous, but such a party must have been in the minority.

In Acarnania, however, there must have been resentment at the loss of Oeniadae. The considerations of Roman power outlined above must have been present to the minds of the Acarnanians as well as to those of the Epirotes, but the entire history of the former people in this period shows that they took a much less "realistic" view of such factors than their northern neighbors. Most importantly, they could not be pro-Roman in any sense if the Romans in the future should resume friendly relations with the Aetolians, the ancient enemies of Acarnania. As long as any such Roman-Aetolian accord persisted, or was renewed, the Acarnanians would never be able to forget that the Romans had been willing to toss Acarnania as bait to Aetolia to secure the latter's friendship.[168]

In fact, generally speaking, Rome was quite unpopular throughout the Greek world in 205 because of her cruel and ferocious methods of war. One scholar[169] goes so far as to say that Rome's campaigns in the east in this war amount to little more than pirate raids, like those of the Illyrians she had suppressed.[170]

Chapter III

THE SECOND MACEDONIAN AND SYRIAN WARS: *AMICITIA* AND CONCILIATION

LESS THAN five years after the Peace of Phoenice the Roman government had determined once more to interfere in Greek affairs. During the course of the new war, the Second Macedonian War, if not before, a majority of the governing classes of the Roman republic seems to have determined to draw Greece into the Roman sphere of influence. In other words, the Roman government embarked upon a policy of active voluntary imperialism in Balkan lands. The system of an informal "protectorate," first originated by the Romans for Illyria, was extended to all Greece in the years following the Second Macedonian War. For Rome's control of Greece no settlement of the country as a formal province with a resident governor was necessary. There had been no resident officials in the Illyrian "protectorate" either.[1] This policy must have existed in 196 B.C., for it is clearly shown in Flamininus' settlement of the affairs of Greece (196/4 B.C.). Therefore it is the logical development of Rome's interpretation of the *senatusconsultum* regulating the affairs of Greece and the combined action of that document and the Isthmian proclamation of 196 in setting the Greeks "free."[2] But in turn the "freedom" of the Greeks is implicit in the Roman ultimatums to Philip and Nicanor in 200 B.C.[3] Those ultimatums commanded Philip's withdrawal from Greece, but his evacuation of that country would create a "power vacuum" there. There were only two possible substitutes for Philip, Antiochus or Rome; and Antiochus was obviously undesirable in the Roman view. Hence it follows that the Roman program for Greece had been evolved, in general terms, at least as early as the beginning of the war.

Nevertheless it is probably correct to hold that the coming of the Second Macedonian War was fortuitous at the time it did come. It is difficult to believe that the majority of the senate would have plunged Rome and Italy into another great war so soon after the conclusion of the Second Punic War, unless it felt that the urgency was great. Hence with regard to the time chosen, but probably not in the sense that the Romans were as yet uninterested in eastern imperialism, Holleaux[4] is right in maintaining that the coming of the Second Macedonian War was accidental.

Not the least of the difficulties involved in a study of the outbreak of the Second Macedonian War is the circumstance that we have no satisfactory straightforward account. Livy's narrative has some truth in it, but is thoroughly confused by a mass of inventions, while Polybius is fragmentary. Holleaux's[5] reconstruction of events may be summarized as follows: Taking advantage of the fact that a minor had succeeded to the throne of Egypt, Philip V and King Antiochus III of Syria entered into a compact[6] to partition the foreign dominions of the new Ptolemy between them. In grabbing off Ptolemy's Aegean possessions (and other, non-Ptolemaic, cities in the Aegean region for good measure), Philip aroused the apprehensions of Rhodes and Pergamum, who went to war with him. Feeling unable to cope with Philip without outside assistance, in the autumn of 201 B.C. the two powers appealed to Rome for help, representing the alliance of Philip and Antiochus as being directed ultimately against Rome. Hence the Roman senate adopted a policy of war, although only a year earlier it had rejected an Aetolian plea[7] for help against the waxing power of Philip V.[8] Undoubtedly significant of the resolution of the senate was the election late in 201 B.C. of P. Sulpicius Galba to the consulate for 200. Galba, having succeeded Laevinus in the east in 210, qualified as a "specialist" in Greco-Macedonian affairs; he received Macedonia as his "province."[9]

Meanwhile, in the east, Philip spent the winter of 201/200 cooped up in the Bay of Bargylia in Asia Minor; but in the spring of 200 he eluded his Rhodian and Pergamene enemies and returned to Macedonia.[10] If hostilities, the cloud in the west, were actually threatening from Italy, it was desirable that Philip be assured that the western members of the Hellenic League, Epirus and Acarnania, were well disposed in his favor. As far as Epirus was concerned, Philip could be fairly sure that the majority of that people would favor his side in a conflict with the Roman barbarian.[11] But Philip's experience with the Epirotes in the First Macedonian War showed him that their sympathy with his cause would probably not extend to active participation in a war against Rome on the Macedonian side. He might expect only their "benevolent neutrality."

The king could also by virtue of his experience in the late war expect that the Acarnanians would actively assist him against Rome. Yet the Acarnanians had suffered considerably for their loyalty to Philip in that war. Very possibly the nucleus of a pro-Roman party was forming in Acarnania already,[12] whether from fear of a possible Roman attack on an Acarnania allied with Philip in the event of another war, or for other reasons. Philip's popularity in Greece at large had suffered quite a check in revulsion from his cruel and savage conduct in the Aegean, his treatment of Cius and Thasos for example.[13] There were probably not wanting those in Acarnania, also, who sharply disapproved.[14]

Hence when Philip returned to Macedonia in the spring of 200 B.C. and found Acarnanian envoys waiting with a request for help against Athens, one of his motives in granting the Acarnanian request may have been to conciliate Acarnanian good will.[15] He was also interested in administering Athens a stinging rebuke for recent manifestations of anti-Macedonian sentiment.

The cause of the Acarnanian grievance was peculiar. In August/September, 201 B.C., two young Acarnanians were detected in the act of profaning the Eleusinian mysteries by their uninitiated presence at the rites. A wave of religious hysteria such as gripped the Athenians from time to time in their history,[16] probably in no small part reinforced by anti-Macedonian feeling, seems to have swept the city, and the culprits were hastily put to death. The next spring (200) the Acarnanians appealed for Philip's aid in procuring vengeance, and a joint Macedonian and Acarnanian force harried Attica with fire and sword and carried off a great deal of booty.[17] About the same time four Athenian warships were seized and carried off by Philip's fleet.[18] Thereupon the Athenians, heartened by the exhortations of King Attalus of Pergamum—himself probably egged on by a Roman embassy then in Athens—declared war on Philip.[19]

At the beginning of the year 200 B.C. the Roman consul Sulpicius proposed to the *comitia* to declare war on Philip and the Macedonians. Virtually all of the centuries voted against the motion.[20] Nevertheless in the spring of the same year an embassy including C. Claudius Nero, M. Aemilius Lepidus, and P. Sempronius Tuditanus was sent to the east. Ostensibly it was intended to convey various courteous messages to the king of Egypt, as well as to arrange a settlement in his war with Antiochus of Syria;[21] actually its prime motive was to survey the situation in Greece and win friends for Rome.[22]

In the early spring of 200 B.C., when the embassy crossed to Greece, the senate had already formulated what was to be at once the pretext for the war and a means of attracting the Greek states to the Roman side—the freedom of Greece. Wherever they halted the envoys informed the Greeks that the Romans were going to demand that Philip make war on no Greek state[23] under penalty of war with Rome. Obviously this would end Macedonian hegemony in any part of Greece and was tantamount to a demand for Greek freedom.[24] The use of such a declaration of policy to win friends in Greece, and even under its cover to rule Greece, was not new. The stratagem was at least as old as the King's Peace of 386 B.C.[25] and had been used repeatedly since that time. But the Romans need not have been studying the history of Greece to discover it. In the First Macedonian War the Aetolians, Roman allies, had proclaimed that the Macedonian kings had enslaved Greece; Aetolia and her allies had obviously been fighting to free Greece from the Macedonian yoke.[26] Evidently the Romans had been impressed with the force of this approach to the Greeks and had adapted it to their own wishes and needs, now that it was convenient for them to do so.

On their way southward, sailing along the Greek coast, the Romans stopped off at Phoenice, which was conveniently located under these circumstances,[27] and communicated their ultimatum to the Epirotes. Later on, as they proceeded eastward, the good news was brought to King Amynander of Athamania, to the Aetolians, and to the Achaeans.[28] Obviously the ultimatum was communicated to those powers on whom it might produce some effect. The attitude of the Epirotes in the First Macedonian War had been so complaisant that it was logical to expect they might continue it in the future. Now that the Romans were determined on a showdown with Philip, the state through which ran an important route to the south and east of Greece acquired increased importance in Roman eyes. Notable, however, is the omission of Acarnania, which manifestly was also conveniently situated on the route of the embassy; but the omission is quite understandable. Despite the *amicitia* which had technically existed between Rome and the Acarnanians since the Peace of Phoenice, the envoys must have been aware that the alliance between Philip and these people had been reaffirmed only a few months before. In any event, since the Romans were desirous of wooing the co-operation of Aetolia, they could not have the friendship of Acarnania as well. Between the military potentials of these two powers there could be no choice.[29] It should also be observed that, all other considerations apart, this announcement of the purpose of the Romans in Greece was equivalent to an invitation to abandon the Hellenic League— at least as far as the Epirotes and Achaeans were concerned.[30] If Philip could not make war on any Greek state, the Hellenic League would be obsolete. Any member of that league, therefore, which agreed to the provisions of the ultimatum agreed also to the dissolution of the league. Unfortunately we do not know what the reception of the news of the ultimatum was. Since we are told, however, that the majority of the Epirotes were favorably disposed to Philip in 198,[31] presumably the implied invitation to leave the Hellenic League was not well received in Epirus generally. Conceivably out of fear of Roman attack the Epirotes, in their exposed position, were well content with a policy of neutrality, but they were not yet ready to leave the league and range themselves upon the side of the barbarian.[32] The harshness of the Romans in the preceding war was not well calculated to win them friends for this one.

Meanwhile the embassy went on to Athens, where it was present at the time of the arrival of Attalus and probably instigated him to persuade the Athenians to declare war on Philip. While the Romans were at Athens, Philip sent an expedition to harry Attica once again, undoubtedly in answer to the Athenian declaration of war. The embassy then presented its demands to Philip's general, Nicanor. Thereafter the envoys proceeded to Rhodes and probably after they had received the news of the declaration of war on Philip by the *comitia* (summer, 200) dispatched Lepidus, the youngest of their number, to the king, who was occupied in besieging the city of Abydus. There in a famous interview Lepidus presented Philip with the Roman ultimatum, which Philip of course rejected.³³ Thus Rome and Macedonia were formally at war for the second time.³⁴

In the autumn of 200 B.C. the consul Sulpicius arrived in Illyria and established himself for the approaching winter in the vicinity of Apollonia, while the fleet made its headquarters at Corcyra.³⁵ Sulpicius spent the winter here in Illyria, but he was not idle. To his camp during that period came various princelings who offered their assistance to the Romans.³⁶ We have no information as to whether or not Sulpicius attempted to get in touch with the Epirotes, or with the pro-Roman faction in Epirus.³⁷ A year later some of the Epirotes were willing to co-operate actively with the Romans, and Apollonia is easy of access from Epirus, not to mention Corcyra. Hence further sounding out of the Epirotes, perhaps to determine the effect of the ultimatum on them, is not impossible. In any event, in 199 Sulpicius decided to try to go directly over the mountains, making a frontal assault on Macedonia. The attempt failed, but the Romans derived sufficient prestige from their penetration of the western reaches of Macedonia to induce the Aetolians to enter the war against Philip.³⁸ If the victory made sufficient impression to bring the Aetolians into the war, it is likely that it raised Roman prestige generally throughout Greece. On the other hand, the failure of Sulpicius to attain his ultimate object must have made it evident to the Epirotes that the Romans might very well choose the alternative route through their country the next year.³⁹

In the fall of 199 P. Villius Tappulus, consul for that year, succeeded Sulpicius as the commander in the east. Next spring (198), however, Philip took the initiative. With the main body of his troops boldly leaving Macedonia, the king marched through part of Epirus and took up a position in the gorges of the Aous to await the coming of the Romans. His position was either in Atintania, part of his own territories since 205, or on its border.⁴⁰ He might shrewdly guess from the campaign of the preceding year what move the Romans would make next, particularly since the Aetolians had come into the war. Presumably the Romans would wish to effect a juncture with the Aetolians. In any event Philip did not run too much danger, for the Romans could be cut off from their base in Apollonia if they moved eastward while Philip was to the south.⁴¹ Villius, meanwhile, had been wintering at Corcyra, when he was informed by Charops, one of the Epirote oligarchs, that Philip had taken up a position on the Aous.[42] We are not told under what circumstances Charops informed Villius of Philip's move. Possibly Charops, in bearing this news to the Roman general, initiated relations with the Romans. Yet it is at least as likely that Villius had been sounding out the Epirotes and trying to win their co-operation in the war. Perhaps it is not without significance that he chose to winter at Corcyra rather than Apollonia, particularly when he had had to quell a mutiny of the land troops the previous autumn.[43] Other things being equal, one would expect a general to remain in the vicinity of his possibly still disaffected troops. Corcyra, however, is little more than a stone's throw from Epirus, and very convenient for discussions with Epirote leaders. At least, Charops was probably the head of the pro-Roman party in Epirus.

Villius brought his army forward and encamped five miles from the Macedonians, but while he was debating whether to attempt to force a passage or to try again the route over the mountains, he was informed that the consul for 198, T. Quinctius Flamininus, had arrived at Corcyra. The new commander had set out for his province with much greater dispatch than usual.[44] From Corcyra Flamininus crossed the narrow strait into Epirus and hastened through Chaonia to the Roman camp in Atintania. He was evidently accompanied by a small escort only, since he pressed on ahead of the eight thousand infantry and eight hundred cavalry which had accompanied him to Corcyra.[45] There is no reason to believe that this was a daring dash through hostile territory; the implication is that the Epirotes had already intimated in some way to the Romans their intention of taking no active part in this war as in the preceding one.

Once in command, Flamininus determined to attempt to force the king's position rather than use the eastward route. Forty days passed in minor battles and skirmishes.[46] Philip chose to take advantage of this impasse to make overtures to the Romans through the Epirotes. Pausanias, the Epirote *strategos,* and Alexander, the hipparch, arranged an interview between Flamininus and Philip. The first demand of Flamininus was that the king withdraw his garrisons from the states (of Greece) and make amends for the damage he had done. In other words, Flamininus reiterated in substance the ultimatum of 200 B.C.: Philip must withdraw from

Greece, which meant in turn that the Hellenic League must be disbanded. The Greeks were to be free of Macedonia. Philip answered that the various states belonged in different categories. Later he asked the consul what states should be freed. Flamininus began by mentioning Thessaly, which had been a subsidiary of the Macedonian crown since the time of Philip II and Alexander. Thus he clearly showed that he intended no compromise, and Philip in anger abruptly broke off the parley.[47]

The resumption of hostilities the next day produced no result, but now Roman negotiations with the Epirotes bore some fruit. Charops sent to the Roman camp the inevitable shepherd, who knew a track in the hills by which Philip's position could be outflanked, Flamininus cautiously checked the shepherd's story by sending to Charops for confirmation. The Epirote replied that the man could be trusted as long as the Romans did not follow him blindly, but kept a firm control of the situation.[48] Flamininus decided to make the attempt.[49] Evidently the Roman believed that Charops was whole-heartedly devoted to the Roman cause. One may assume that Charops had not sent the shepherd to the consul previously because the Epirote oligarch had only recently learned of the existence of the path.

After some hesitation, then, owing to his misgiving about the advisability of trusting the shepherd, as was natural in view of Charops' qualified endorsement of the latter, Flamininus sent a detachment along the path the shepherd indicated. The main Roman army attacked on sighting the smoke signal which informed it that the special detachment had accomplished its mission. The Macedonian forces were compelled to retreat headlong, and Philip retired to Thessaly.[50] For the time being the Romans did not follow the king; it was important not to leave Epirus until the Roman lines of communication through the country were secure.

It was also desirable to secure a port farther south for the Roman supply ships in order to avoid the difficulty and costly transport by land through the mountains of Epirus. Aetolian Ambracia was selected for the purpose;[51] indeed, it was better situated from the Roman point of view than the Acarnanian port of Leucas, which Flamininus may have tried to win over. At any rate, after he had proceeded to Thessaly he was uncertain whether the supply ships had sailed to Ambracia or Leucas.[52] This may mean that Flamininus had thought that Philip's dislodgement from the Aous and the Romans' exemplary conduct in Epirus (as well as Acarnanian fear of the Roman fleet) might induce the Leucadians to come over to the Roman side. If this is so, Flamininus may have offered the Leucadians his friendship and been rebuffed. Certainly most of them were hostile a year later. In any event, it is difficult to see why the Roman supply ships might proceed to Leucas unless they had received tentative instructions to do so. Yet Leucas was a member of the Acarnanian League, known to be hostile to Rome. Perhaps Flamininus underrated its hostility and hence had to change the orders of the supply ships at the last moment. But this in turn means he had been informed that the climate of public opinion at Leucas was too unfriendly to the Romans[53] to permit the easy landing of the supply ships there. Finally he may have learned from the Epirotes or the Aetolians that Ambracia, with its difficult but short route to Thessaly, was better situated for his purpose,[54] with the additional advantage of being in friendly Aetolian hands. Yet active hostility of the Leucadians could seriously hamper Roman supply ships sailing to Ambracia, the entrance to whose gulf was commanded by the island of Leucas. Possibly the consul relied on fear of the Roman fleet to deter the Leucadians from an open attack on the supply ships; possibly also he counted on the pro-Roman faction in Acarnania[55] to thwart such a project. Hence presumably Flamininus redirected the supply ships to Ambracia, but was later concerned as to whether or not they had received the new orders.

Meanwhile Flamininus well knew that the pro-Roman party in Epirus was quite small; yet it must have been fairly numerous, for many Epirotes were willing to join the Roman auxiliaries as guides,[56] and the Romans were evidently willing to trust them. In order to conciliate the inhabitants of the country,[57] no plundering was allowed in Epirus. The soldiers had to put up with the fairly scanty rations that could be purchased, and the army conducted itself generally with admirable discipline.[58] The neutrality of the Epirotes was thus meticulously observed.[59] Having thus occupied himself approximately a month[60] in conciliating the Epirotes and securing his communications with the west, Flamininus at last followed Philip across the mountains into Thessaly.[61]

During the rest of the summer and the early autumn the Romans extended their sway over central and southern Greece. One of their most important accomplishments was the winning over of the Achaeans to their side by judicious use of persuasion and an implied threat of force. Philip, however, was yet to be met in a pitched battle and defeated. Flamininus, therefore, unsure whether his command would be prorogued for the next year, and desirous of winning the glory of terminating the war himself, was willing to negotiate with the king.[62] Accordingly another conference was arranged, to be held on the shores of the Malian Gulf near Nicaea.[63] The detailed account of these negotiations need not concern us here. Flamininus spoke first and demanded that Philip withdraw from the whole of Greece and that he surrender those districts of Illyria which had been ceded to him by the treaty made in Epirus, *i.e.*, the Peace of Phoenice.[64] The territories thus designated included Atintania.[65] That Philip withdraw from the whole of Greece was also the general desire of all the powers associated with Rome in the war.[66] Philip was willing to make many concessions, but not to yield this much. For his own reasons, Flamininus then referred Philip to the senate. An armistice of two months was arranged for the purpose; but the senate answered Philip's envoys by saying, in effect, that the king must withdraw from all Greece, when it asked them whether Macedonia were ready to yield the "fetters of Greece," Chalcis, Demetrias, Corinth. The war, therefore, continued, and the command of Flamininus was prorogued.[67] Thus the Roman government (albeit with some personal tergiversations on the part of Flamininus) simply reiterated the program it had had in 200: the withdrawal of Philip from Greece, which in turn meant the end of the Hellenic League. That organization, however, was virtually derelict by this time anyway, since the Achaeans, its most important single member, had gone over to the Romans, and Roman authority had been asserted in various ways over most of the members in central Greece. Acarnania almost alone still adhered to its alliance with Philip;[68] the continued allegiance of the Epirotes was a mere formality which would shortly evaporate at Cynoscephalae and the following peace.

It was desirable that Acarnania, located so strategically on the Roman lines of communication with eastern Greece, be brought over to the Roman side. It is uncertain to what extent the Acarnanians were co-operating with Philip at this time. In 197

Acarnanians were to be found in the king's forces,[69] but these might have been mercenaries. Yet the Acarnanians were potential enemies, and in the event of a Roman reverse might make their hostility felt with devastating effect. In the fall of 198 Flamininus considered wintering in Acarnania, but abandoned the idea because there was no port there which could accommodate both the supply fleet and the army.[70] Very possibly it had occurred to Flamininus that the presence of Roman troops with the implied threat of force which they would constitute might bring the country over into the Roman camp, much as fear of the fleet had influenced the decision of the Achaeans and as, later, a judicious and timely display of force intimidated Boeotia.[71]

At the end of the winter of 197 Flamininus dispatched his brother Lucius to the west to attempt to seduce the Acarnanians away from their allegiance to Philip.[72] Lucius proceeded to Corcyra, the headquarters of the fleet, of which he had command this year. To the island Lucius summoned the chief men among the Acarnanians, with whom he made some progress in achieving his end. The Acarnanians, however, had now been the faithful allies of Macedonia for over a generation. Only three years earlier that alliance had protected their interests, or gratified their spleen. But the chief thing that made them reluctant to abandon their allegiance to Philip and join the Roman side was their fear of the Aetolians, now the principal Greek combatants on the Roman side. Nevertheless, we may suppose that Lucius and the chief pro-Roman leaders, including probably the league *strategos* as well as other magistrates, evolved a plan which aimed at shanghaiing the *koinon* into the Roman camp. An assembly of the league was summoned to meet at Leucas, the capital. Not all of the members of the *koinon* were represented there. Why, we have no certain means of knowing. Possibly the pro-Roman party tampered with the machinery for summoning the meeting; if so, the meeting was probably a special one. Presumably those regions where anti-Roman feeling was strongest were not notified, or not notified in time. At the rump meeting two magistrates (this perhaps explains the possible tampering with the convocation procedure) passed a "privatum decretum" to place the Acarnanians on the Roman side, although even in such a gathering they could not make the decree unanimous. The meaning of the expression "private decree" or "unofficial decree" is uncertain. Conceivably the fact that not all member states were represented affected the decree's character, or there may well have been some other defect of procedure. In any event the decree was not without some validity, for it was necessary to rescind it later.

The unrepresented states bitterly resented this attempt to force a *fait accompli* down their throats. Some time must have elapsed, for Livy implies that Philip stimulated two Acarnanians of his way of thinking to take action. These two men were able not only to procure the revocation of the decree favoring Rome, but to convict of treason the two men who had proposed the decree and to depose the *strategos* on the ground that he had put an illegal motion. Although the two convicted traitors were advised to flee to Corcyra, they boldly appeared in the assembly and were able to persuade that body to revoke their sentence. On the other hand, the assembly resolved firmly to abide by its alliance with Philip.[73] The fact that the two pro-Roman schemers were able to escape unscathed probably indicates that the pro-Roman party in Acarnania in 197 — or at least those who feared Roman retribution — was, while less than a majority, still a sizable minority. The pro-Roman party's attempt to use a rump assembly to achieve its purpose points to the same thing.

His attempt to produce a "voluntary" conciliation of the Acarnanians having misfired in this fashion, Lucius now resorted to force. Sailing to Leucas, he placed the city under siege; and although the inhabitants resisted with desperate valor, the Romans were finally able to take the city through the treachery of some Italian exiles who admitted the besiegers. A few days after the city's fall news came of Cynoscephalae (June, 197), and all of Acarnania surrendered to Lucius.[74] Livy says that the Acarnanians "in dicionem legati venerunt."[75] In other words the Acarnanians performed a legal act which the Romans, at least, interpreted as *deditio*, for *venire in dicionem* is an alternative expression for *se dedere*.[76] Thus the last member of the Hellenic League capitulated to overwhelming force.[77]

Shortly after the battle of Cynoscephalae, the decisive victory which the Romans wanted, Philip offered peace on the basis of the demands of the Romans and their associates in the "former conference."[78] This must mean the conference of Nicaea of the previous autumn. Although neither the written statement of the demands of his enemies presented to Philip on that occasion,[79] nor the treaty ratified at Rome,[80] has been preserved, the general tenor of the treaty can be deduced from the demands made by the Romans and their associates during the course of that conference.[81] Accordingly, among other provisions, the treaty of peace ordered Philip to surrender to the Romans Atintania and the other portions of the Illyrian "protectorate" which he had annexed after 205 by virtue of the treaty of Phoenice, and to withdraw from Greece.[82] It is important to note also that the Romans regarded the peace as being between themselves and Philip. It was their peace, and the other powers associated with them in Greece could, in colloquial terminology, "like it or lump it."[83]

At the end of the winter or the beginning of the spring of 196[84] ten commissioners from Rome arrived in Greece to assist Flamininus in settling the affairs of that country, bearing with them the *senatusconsultum* designed to implement the peace treaty.[85] This document contained the following provisions relevant to the present discussion: "All the rest of the Greeks in Asia and Europe were to be free and subject to their own laws; Philip was to surrender to the Romans before the Isthmian games those Greeks subject to his rule and the cities in which he had garrisons...."[86] In other words, the Greek states subject to Philip and the cities in which he had garrisons were to be handed over to the Romans; Rome declared that all the other Greeks of Asia and Europe were free.

The Aetolians, already disgruntled with Roman conduct, claimed that the clause about the places surrendered to the Romans meant that the latter were merely substituting themselves for the Macedonians as the masters of Greece.[87] Flamininus, therefore, persuaded the ten commissioners that it was necessary to convince the Greeks that Rome's real motive in the war had been the promotion of Greek liberty. It must be announced that the places in question, especially Corinth, Chalcis, and Demetrias, were to be set free. The commissioners finally agreed to this proposal, albeit reluctantly; they had received instructions at Rome regarding the other matters connected with the settlement, but the question of these three places had been left to their own decision, "because of Antiochus."[88] Since the Isthmian games, an occasion when Greeks from all quarters would be present, were conveniently at hand (May/June),[89] it was decided to clear up the rumors rife throughout the country with the following proclamation made on that occasion:

> The senate of Rome, and Titus Quintius the proconsul having overcome King Philip and the Macedonians, leave the following peoples free, without garrisons and subject to no tribute and governed by their countries' laws — the Corinthians, Phocians, Locrians, Euboeans, Phthiotic Achaeans, Magnesians, Thessalians, and Perrhaebians.[90]

The states mentioned in the proclamation were states which had been in one way or another subject to Philip's rule or hegemony in the late war. Some of them were members of the Hellenic League; viz., the Phocians, possibly the Locrians, the Euboeans, and the Thessalians with their one-time subject peoples now treated separately — the Phthiotic Achaeans, Magnesians, and Perrhaebians. Rome, moreover, had engaged in military action against many of them during the war.

The states of Epirus and Acarnania were affected both by the treaty with Philip and by the *senatusconsultum*. The treaty, ordering Philip to withdraw from Greece, dissolved the Hellenic League and thus severed the alliance between Philip and Epirus. The *senatusconsultum*, by declaring the Greeks of Europe free, confirmed Rome's previous *de facto* recognition of the neutrality and freedom of Epirus. The surrender of Acarnania had already effectively ended her connection with the Hellenic League. Yet her case is a bit more involved. Acarnania had been a member of the league, but more importantly she had also borne arms against the Romans and surrendered.[91] One would expect that the Acarnanians should therefore be mentioned in the Isthmian proclamation, as they would seem to fall in the same category as the states there enumerated. But, since the Acarnanians are not so mentioned, they too must be regarded as coming under the operation of the *senatusconsultum*, as being declared free and subject to their own laws.

Yet Leucas had been seized and occupied by the troops of Lucius Flamininus in 197. If the status of Acarnania in June, 196, had still been the same as it had been at the time of its capitulation in June, 197, it would have been incumbent on Titus Flamininus to have mentioned Acarnania in the proclamation. If the status of

Acarnania in 196 were the same as that of 197, the omission of her name from the proclamation would have been a very glaring indication that the Romans did not intend to let the Acarnanians go free. Since that would have defeated the object of the proclamation, which was to scotch Aetolian rumors that the Romans were trying to become masters of Greece, it is surprising that Acarnania was not mentioned.[92] The omission of Acarnania from the proclamation must mean that the status of that country at the time of the Isthmian games was clear beyond dispute; in other words, that some action had been taken to show that Leucas and Acarnania were free. The easiest and most obvious way would have been merely to withdraw the Roman forces from the territories of the *koinon*. But such an action might have been dangerous, for the Aetolians were eager to gain possession of Leucas and might have attempted a *coup de main*.[93] Hence Lucius Flamininus seems to have retained his base on the island; at least he appears to have been quartered there in 195.[94] Accordingly we must postulate that Titus Flamininus or the commissioners must have made some sort of declaration that Leucas and Acarnania were to be free and "use their own laws"; or that they performed some act tantamount to the same thing. It was of course quite possible for the most favorable legal status to follow upon *deditio*.[95]

The commissioners had instructions covering the settlement of Greece except for the status of Corinth, Chalcis, and Demetrias. Their instructions, then, must have included Acarnania, whether by a specific provision or by some general clause. This must mean either that the recognition of Acarnanian freedom was made shortly after the commissioners' arrival in Greece (late winter/early spring 196), or that Flamininus had taken the necessary steps previously and the senate had confirmed his action.

It was convenient for the Aetolians in the years 196/4 B.C. to claim that the treaty of 211 was still in force. If this were admitted, they should be permitted to occupy all places captured by the Romans. Obviously, it was equally convenient for the Romans to deny the Aetolian contention. Leucas fell in the category of places to which the Aetolians might lay claim under the arrangements of 211;[96] and they did not hesitate to urge that it be handed over to them when the commissioners and Flamininus got down to the details of settling the affairs of Greece. Their request was referred to the senate,[97] but the senate referred it back to Flamininus.[98] This was almost certainly equivalent to a refusal,[99] and Leucas remained in Acarnanian hands.[100]

It seems obvious that both the Epirotes and the Acarnanians were treated in the war and in the settlement with particular leniency.[101] Moreover, although Flamininus interfered regularly and frequently in the affairs of the other Greek states involved in the settlement,[102] he did not, so far as we know, do so in either Epirus or Acarnania. This, too, has some importance as indicating the status of these two powers, for interference of a great power in the internal affairs of smaller powers regularly means the beginning of control.[103] From this period until the age of the late republic, when Roman rule of Greece was a matter of course, Rome concluded very few formal treaties with Greek states. The settlement after the Second Macedonian War produced alliances only with Macedonia and Achaea. Most Greek states which sided with Rome in that war and thereafter did so only on the basis of an informal understanding. Epirus and Acarnania were, it seems, placed in this category, although the former had been strictly neutral in the war just over and the latter had been actively hostile.[104] It looks, therefore, as though the Romans desired these two states to be free insofar as was possible, or insofar as any small power could hope to be in relation to a state whose might was relatively so overwhelming as was Rome's. "It looks like a deliberate plan to win by conciliation those states of northwest Greece that at the same time were relatively accessible to the Romans and important to them if intervention in Greece again should become necessary."[105] The two powers together constituted for the Romans their principal and nearest entrance to the Greek east. Accordingly, the unexpectedly lenient treatment meted out to both of them, especially to Acarnania, renders fairly safe the assumption that the Romans saw in Epirus and Acarnania special circumstances. Such circumstances could only be geographical; neither state was a great power.[106] At least as long as Rome had any doubts of her ability to crush any eastern great power, she might calculate that the defection of these two states would prove embarrassing. Therefore she wooed their voluntary allegiance by every means at her command.

Legally, after 197/6 the status of Acarnania in the eyes of Rome was one of *amicitia* or *societas*. In succeeding years the Acarnanians are called "socii" of the Romans,[107] but this is no ground for believing that they had become "allies," *foederati* of the Romans,[108] for *socius* and *amicus* are frequently interchangeable terms.[109] Nor is there any reason to suppose that the Epirotes received a *foedus;* they retained their old status as *socii* or *amici.*[110]

In all probability, therefore, Epirote and Acarnanian representatives were included in the meetings of all the *socii* with Flamininus at Corinth in 195 to discuss relations with Nabis,[111] and in 194 to hear Flamininus' farewell address.[112] Possibly also the two northwestern powers contributed contingents to the war against Nabis.[113] Relevant here is a very obscure passage in Livy,[114] who says that in 192 the Achaean statesman Philopoemen summoned a council of Achaeans and *socii* to meet at Tegea to deal with the problem of Nabis, and that there were leading men of the Epirotes and Acarnanians present at that meeting. This passage has been interpreted by Benedictus Niese[115] to mean that the Epirotes and Acarnanians attended that meeting by virtue of their status as Roman *socii*. This must be incorrect. The passage clearly implies that *socii* should be taken in conjunction with the Achaeans.[116] Since, then, we are not dealing with *socii* as applied technically to Roman "associates," the natural assumption would seem to be that the two powers were allies of the Achaeans.[117] Yet it has recently been suggested that *socii* does refer to Roman *socii,* that the Achaeans had invited the states "associated" with Rome to participate in the meeting, and that the particular mention of these two peoples means that they alone replied favorably to the invitation. This is an attractive suggestion,[118] but unfortunately the same objection raised against Niese's theory is valid here. It seems difficult to believe that Livy (whose source here is Polybius) would not have specified the *socii Romanorum,* if such he meant, when otherwise the context clearly implies *socii* of the Achaeans. Livy was writing a history of Rome, and if Rome's "associates" were meant he should have mentioned it. Livy does not say that only these two other powers were represented; there might well be some other reason for special mention of these two, a reason which Livy's source, Polybius, made clear, but which Livy, abridging something which was not directly connected with the history of Rome, has omitted.[119]

Epirus and Acarnania were thus *amici* of Rome after 197/6, as the former had been uninterruptedly since 205. How much real "friendship" was there for Rome in these states? In conciliating the real allegiance of these peoples, as of the Greeks generally, the Romans labored under certain disadvantages. First of all they were barbarians, and on that account alone their waxing influence in Hellas was distasteful to the Greeks;[120] the harshness of Roman war-making was also repellent to the Greeks,[121] certainly including the Epirotes and Acarnanians. On the other hand, those peoples, like most Greek states of the time, were ruled by oligarchies. In Epirus certainly,[122] and in Acarnania as well, although perhaps to a lesser extent, the ruling classes had reason to fear the class unrest in Greece. Situated as they were, on the main route to Italy which was traveled by numerous merchants from both east and west, the two powers were in an excellent position to observe the traditional support given by Rome, herself an oligarchy,[123] to the better classes in areas under her hegemony. The settlement of Greek affairs in 196 by the Romans, regularly in favor of the ruling classes, confirmed the impression, if any confirmation were needed.[124] For that reason there was naturally a distinct tendency for the ruling classes in Greece to support the Romans in their guise as proponents of the existing economic and social order[125] and, logically, for the lower classes to be anti-Roman.[126] As the corollary to this situation, for some years before the Second Macedonian War Philip, for whatever primary motives, had frequently acted in a manner which could easily be interpreted as favoring the lower classes.[127] Nevertheless, it would be easy to exaggerate the importance of this aspect of Greco-Roman relationships.[128] It forms only one aspect of power politics. Flamininus did not boggle at allying with Nabis, the arch-advocate of social revolution in Greece, as long as it was politically and militarily expedient to do so. Likewise there were other considerations which influenced the Acarnanians and Epirotes to favor the Roman side. Primary, from this point of view, was the overwhelming force at Rome's disposal, coupled with the extraordinarily exposed position of the two powers. These factors combined to produce, from the beginning in Epirus, by 197 in Acarnania, a party which probably was not so much "pro-Roman" for the most part, as more or less sullenly acquiescent under Roman domination. Really devoted pro-Romans were probably fairly rare— as is, one is tempted to say, the heart-and-soul quisling at all times.[129] How much the short-lived Roman conciliatory policy was able to induce a change in this attitude after 197/6 our scanty sources do not allow us to say. It would also be hard to say to what extent the oligarchs in the two states were favorably impressed by Rome's pro-oligarchic policy, but it would be rash to deny that policy any influence in determining the attitude of men like Charops.

In 194 the Romans completely evacuated their troops and officials from Greece. In 192, however, a new war began in the east, the war of the Romans against the Aetolians and Antiochus. The latter, probably wishing merely to regain the former possessions of his house in Europe, had occupied several cities of Thrace in 196.[130] The Romans, possibly sincerely alarmed at this near approach of Antiochus to their own sphere of influence in Greece, at once protested to the Great King. A series of diplomatic maneuvers and conferences followed, producing no settlement of the question. Meanwhile the Aetolians, exasperated by their failure to receive much of what they had expected after the war with Philip, pressed the Seleucid to join them in liberating Greece from the Romans. The Lacedaemonian tyrant, Nabis, was also restive under the peace which had been imposed upon him by Flamininus. It was to deal with the problem posed by Nabis' renewed hostility that leading men of Epirus and Acarnania met with the Achaeans at Tegea in 192.[131] Finally in the autumn of that year Antiochus crossed to Greece with ten thousand foot and five hundred horse,[132] and in the following winter war was formally declared upon him and his accomplices by the *comitia* at Rome.[133]

As had been the case in the war with Philip, however, the Roman government had not waited for this formality to begin operations in Greece against the enemy. Early in 192 Flamininus and three other envoys were sent to Greece to keep in line as many wavering *socii* as possible.[134] There is no record of any activities of this embassy in Epirus or Acarnania[135] until 191, but probably somewhat later in 192 a fleet was sent "to Greece" under the command of A. Atilius Serranus.[136] Possibly it was thought that the presence of this armament would have a salutary effect on the minds of the Epirotes and Acarnanians, especially since it was probably based at Corcyra, like most Roman fleets in the wars in the east at this period. In the autumn of 192 the praetor M. Baebius crossed with a small vanguard to Apollonia.[137] During the ensuing winter Philip met with Baebius in the land of the Illyrian Dassaretii. The two came to an accord which probably included an arrangement that the Romans in this war, with the co-operation of Philip, should use the direct route across Pindus into Greece, instead of the more southerly one through Epirus.[138]

Meanwhile Antiochus was not idle at Chalcis, where he spent most of the winter.[139] His agents were at work in Acarnania,[140] for example, and the king was occupied in returning tactful answers to embassies from Greek states anxious to be on the right side.[141] Hither came no less a person than Charops of Epirus, to ask him not to involve that country in the war with Rome, in view of its situation, so exposed to Roman attack. On the other hand, Charops announced that the Epirotes were willing to receive the king's forces in their cities and harbors, if he was able to protect them. Antiochus answered noncommittally that he would send envoys to the Epirotes to discuss their joint interests.[142] To this account of Polybius Livy adds some additional interpretation. It is uncertain whether this represents Livy's own reflections on the account of Polybius, or *contaminatio* with another source. Alternatively the interpretation may be that of Polybius himself, and it may be that the editors of the extracts which are our source for these fragments of Polybius have abridged him here. At any rate, the additions found in Livy are worthy of attention. In the first place, according to Livy, this embassy was sent by the general consent of the (Epirote) people — "communi gentis consensu." This is quite plausible. We have seen that there is no reason to suppose that the Epirotes generally were genuinely attached to Rome. Livy also says that the object of the Epirotes was to keep a foot in both camps; to conciliate the favor of the king and at the same time, if the king did come to Epirus (which they didn't really expect), to be able to avoid the displeasure of the Romans by pleading the presence of superior force and the absence of the Romans. Whatever may be the source of this interpretation — and it would be no discredit to Polybius — it sums up the real meaning of the embassy with great verisimilitude. The Epirotes were simply trying to follow the policy which they had adopted consistently since the Social War — to avoid the hazards of being caught in the middle of a struggle between great powers in Greece. In other words, the Epirotes were bent on remaining neutral and were willing to use any device which might procure that end. What they would do, should both the Romans and Antiochus appear in force in their country at the same time, is not stated. Probably they hoped not to have to meet that contingency. If it should come about, they might be able by treachery to aid the side which appeared the stronger at the moment, as Charops had done in 198. The incident, finally, shows that not even Charops was really attached to the Roman cause. All he wanted, primarily, was peace at any price. We should interpret his aid to the Romans in 198, then, merely as indicating that he was more astute than most of his fellow-citizens. That early, if not before, he had concluded that Rome had the stronger battalions. If things came to a showdown between the Romans and the Great King in Epirus, he might well come to the same conclusion; but in any event it was better to be prepared for other possibilities as well. Evidently the Roman policy of conciliation in Epirus had not produced any devoted friends and admirers as yet.

The same policy probably had not effected much better results to the south in Acarnania. In that country the agents of Antiochus had won over by bribes a certain Mnasilochus, apparently a citizen of the Acarnanian town of Medion.[143] During the winter of 192/1 Mnasilochus was industriously at work trying[144] to bring the Acarnanians over to the side of the Great King. One of those whom he won over to the anti-Roman party was Clytus, the *strategos* (*praetor*) of the league. In Leucas itself, the capital of Acarnania, Mnasilochus' efforts to provoke a declaration in favor of Antiochus failed, mainly because the Leucadians, mindful of their fate in 197, feared being exposed to the vengeance of the Roman fleet, at that time cruising in the waters off Cephallenia (hence the time was early spring). Therefore Mnasilochus was driven to resort to treachery. Rising at a meeting of the Acarnanian *concilium* which was deliberating the proper course of action to take against Antiochus and his Aetolian allies, he proposed that the entire Acarnanian levy be sent to guard Medion and Thyrrheum to prevent their capture by the Great King and the Aetolians. Apparently in accordance with a prearranged plan, members of the anti-Roman faction argued that the emergency was not sufficiently grave to warrant so drastic a measure and that a force of five hundred would be sufficient for the purpose. This sentiment prevailed, and Mnasilochus procured the dispatch of three hundred men to Medion and two hundred to

Thyrrheum to garrison these towns. It was his plan to deliver these troops into the hands of the king to serve as hostages.[145]

In the meantime, at the beginning of spring, Antiochus had marched westward to Aetolia, where he held a conference with the leaders of his allies. A detachment of the king's troops was commanded by Alexander, an Acarnanian *condottiere*.[146] Presumably from Aetolia the king sent ambassadors ahead to Medion to ask the people of that city to accept his friendship. The local assembly debated the question, and the citizens seemed equally divided, some wishing to abide by the friendship of the Romans, others to accept that of the king. Clytus the *strategos*, perhaps himself a citizen of Medion, recommended sending an embassy to the king, asking that Medion be granted time to refer the matter to the league *concilium*. This advice was followed, but the faction of Antiochus was able to procure the appointment of Mnasilochus and others of the same views to serve on the embassy. Meanwhile the king's friends on the embassy were urging him to advance upon the city with haste, while they themselves deliberately procrastinated on one excuse or another. Hardly had the envoys set out, therefore, before Antiochus was at the city gates. In the general panic which ensued Clytus and Mnasilochus let the king into the city. Both those who were members of the king's party and those who, remembering the frequent course of *stasis* in a Greek city, were compelled by fear joined Antiochus. The Great King diplomatically reassured the panic-stricken populace. Thereupon several Acarnanian communities came over to him voluntarily.

From Medion the king marched toward Thyrrheum, sending Mnasilochus ahead. The latter city, however, warned by the example of Medion, closed its gates against him and announced that it would form no new alliance without the consent of the Roman commander. The wavering Acarnanians were now reassured by Flamininus who sent one of his fellow-ambassadors, Cn. Octavius, to Leucas, to inform the Acarnanians that the new consul, M'. Acilius Glabrio, was already in Greece with a Roman field army. This was plausible, since the sea was now open for sailing; the rest of the Acarnanians held firm, and Antiochus, leaving garrisons at Medion and other places which had surrendered to him, left his position before the walls of Thyrrheum and returned to Chalcis.[147]

Obviously most of the Acarnanians had not declared for Antiochus.[148] Probably the appearance of Seleucid symbols on the coinage of Acarnania at this time[149] represents propaganda of the pro-Seleucid magistrates, more than allegiance of Acarnania to the Great King. It is by no means impossible that Antiochus' alliance with the Aetolians did nothing to raise his credit with the Acarnanians. On the other hand, just as obviously, the allegiance of the Acarnanians to the Roman cause was primarily to be credited to the Roman fleet and to the announced presence of a major Roman army in the Balkans.

What were the motives of Antiochus in this western expedition? It is quite likely that he desired to gratify the Aetolians and gain their confidence,[150] but the most probable reason why the Aetolians and the king should desire to secure Acarnania at this particular juncture must have been the apprehension that the Romans might use Acarnania as a base of operations against them. What more desirable strategy to defeat the Romans than to meet them in the west of the peninsula where they would disembark? Hannibal had advised the king as early as 193[151] to hold his forces in Greece as though prepared to cross to Italy. Northwestern Greece would of course be the obvious choice for such a purpose. Again in the winter of 192/1 Hannibal recommended that Antiochus proceed to Bullis in southern Illyria to offer the appearance of being about to cross to Italy, and actually perhaps to cross, if the opportunity arose. Meanwhile his fleet should be sent to Corcyra to guard the waters off the coasts of Epirus and Illyria.[152] It is not necessary here to enter into the vexed question whether Hannibal's main plan, the invasion of Italy, was feasible or not. Antiochus, at any rate, did not attempt it, for whatever reason. But one of his wisest possible moves would have been to secure the coasts and waters of the Balkans opposite southern Italy. On land it would be impossible to go from Thessaly directly to Epirus, leaving a possibly hostile Acarnania to serve as a base for the Romans to cut him off from his communications with the Aegean. If Antiochus were to follow Hannibal's plan to station himself in the west, he must begin with the seizure of Acarnania; then Epirus could be brought over and he could safely wait for the Romans in the plains of Apollonia where he might be able to drive them into the sea. If he failed there, he could fall back upon eastern Greece for another stand, before being forced back into his own dominions. It looks very much as though Antiochus had been struck by the merits of this part of Hannibal's plan when the latter expounded his views in the council held at Demetrias in the winter of 192/1. He may well have underestimated the fear which the Acarnanians felt of the Roman fleet, and overestimated the strength of the anti-Roman faction in that country. Had Antiochus succeeded in winning Acarnania, it is probable that the ambassadors which the king had promised the winter before to send to Epirus would have made a prompt appearance there with the king at their heels. As things actually turned out, in addition to Antiochus' failure in Acarnania two things primarily conspired against his plan: Philip's agreement with Baebius which permitted the Romans to outflank the Great King by using the direct Pindus route to Thessaly, and the promptitude of Glabrio's action in crossing the Adriatic in force at the earliest possible moment in 191. As it was, Antiochus had lost little; he at once hastened back to eastern Greece from Acarnania, where he could not remain when the Romans were in Thessaly without grave peril of being cut off in a corner. The whole affair well illustrates the strategic value of these two countries in any war between a Balkan and an Italian power.

Later on that same spring Antiochus was defeated by Glabrio at Thermopylae and forced hastily to evacuate Greece. Thereupon Glabrio in conjunction with Philip turned upon the Aetolians, but capturing their cities one by one proved an arduous task. After the Aetolians had surrendered by *deditio,* and then learned the meaning which the Romans attached to their act, and resumed the war, Flamininus finally managed to negotiate a truce.

Meanwhile the Epirotes were uneasily conscious that their conduct had not been beyond misunderstanding, to put the kindest face on it. Evidently their negotiations with Antiochus had not been kept secret. Therefore the Epirote government sent envoys to Glabrio to explain away its conduct. They had departed from the good faith of their *amicitia* with Rome; but they had sent no troops to Antiochus,[153] they said. They were accused (probably falsely) of sending money to Antiochus, but they could not deny that they had sent him ambassadors. When the envoys petitioned for the continuation of their former *amicitia,* the consul answered that he did not know whether they were enemies or were at peace with Rome; he referred them to the senate, granting a truce of ninety days for the purpose. An embassy from Epirus was therefore sent to the senate at Rome. Before that body the Epirotes limited themselves mainly to declaring the various kinds of hostile acts they had not performed. The senate seems to have returned them the type of ambiguous answer which in the next decade it all too frequently gave: the Epirotes were given to understand that their offenses were pardoned, but not that they had been absolved of any hostile intent toward Rome (winter, 191/90).[154] Evidently the Epirotes were kept on tenterhooks for a time to let sink in the lesson which the Romans wished to inculcate: *amici* of Rome might not engage in any foreign policy contrary to Roman wishes and interests. And for the future the Epirotes could reflect that they had been paroled rather acquitted. The Acarnanians of Thyrrheum had already perceived this fundamental principle of concord with Rome, when they replied to Antiochus that they would form no new alliance without the consent of Rome's representatives.[155] In return for her conciliatory treatment of Epirus and Acarnania in 198/7 Rome expected full compliance with her own interpretation of *amicitia* in Greece. It is no wonder that the Greeks had difficulty in understanding the technical aspects of Roman foreign policy. *Amicitia* was evidently a very elastic conception. *Amicitia* in regions where Rome was not interested in maintaining her hegemony was evidently simply a friendly relationship, as in the case of Athens in 228 B.C. Yet the same term meant subservience to Roman foreign policy when Rome chose to interpret it so.

In the early spring of 190 the new consul, L. Cornelius Scipio, accompanied by his more famous and more competent brother, the great Africanus, arrived in Greece. Africanus, eager to be off after Antiochus, promptly arranged a new six months' truce with the Aetolians.[156] As a result the campaigning season of 190 was a relatively quiet one in Greece proper. In midwinter 190/89 Antiochus was defeated at Magnesia in Asia and sued for peace shortly thereafter. Meanwhile the six months' truce in Greece expired without the Aetolians being able to elicit any more favorable terms for themselves at Rome. Consequently, in the winter the Aetolians resumed their war against Philip.

In the spring of 189 B.C. the consul, M. Fulvius Nobilior, crossed with an army to Apollonia.[157] Here he was met by an Epirote delegation which advised him to attack Ambracia. Evidently the

Epirotes were trying to do two things at once: atone for their mistake of 192/1, and very possibly gain Ambracia for themselves into the bargain.[158] During this year the Epirotes considered themselves at war with the Aetolians;[159] when they first considered themselves at war is not specified, but Nobilior's arrival furnished a likely occasion. Otherwise the Epirotes would have been exposed to Aetolian attack without Roman forces to help them. The consul accepted the advice of the ambassadors and marched through Epirus to Ambracia, to which he laid siege.[160] The Epirotes contributed some military assistance.[161]

Whether or not the Epirote hopes of gaining Ambracia were to be fulfilled, they had plans for making pecuniary gain out of their war with Aetolia. In despair at the prospect of fighting a major Roman army after the defeat of Antiochus had removed all possible hope of a diversion, the Aetolians resolved to send still another embassy, consisting of five men, to Rome. On their way these were captured at sea off Cephallenia by a pirate or privateer[162] and brought to Epirus, where they were held for ransom of five talents each — later reduced to three, as time passed and the Epirotes became fearful that the Romans would demand the release of envoys on their way to the senate. This eventually happened, but only after four of the five had paid their three talents. Presumably the Epirotes were not compelled to disgorge their twelve talents. It was to be their only real gain in the war — aside from the doubtful good will of Rome.[163]

The Aetolians could not hope to resist the might of Rome singlehanded, and the Acarnanians[164] and Macedonians were also at war with them. Utilizing the good offices of various neutral powers, Ambracia finally capitulated, and preliminary terms of peace were arranged with Nobilior.[165] A final, detailed treaty of peace was subsequently (189) drawn up and ratified at Rome.[166] By this peace, since all places taken by the Romans since 192 were to be renounced by the Aetolians,[167] Ambracia was lost to the Aetolian *koinon*. It was later made a free city-state, although it might not levy *portoria* on Romans and Latins (187).[168]

Acarnania had been at war with the Aetolians, at the latest since 191, and had suffered from Aetolian raids in 189.[169] For their part the Acarnanians had ambushed some Aetolian ambassadors and confined them at Thyrrheum, whither Nobilior wrote to send the unfortunate diplomats to him.[170] The life of an Aetolian in the foreign service in 189 seems to have been quite adventurous. At any rate, the Acarnanians, unlike the Epirotes, benefited by the peace treaty. By its terms the city of Oeniadae, lost to them since 211 B.C.,[171] was taken from the Aetolians and returned to the Acarnanian *koinon*. Possibly in addition it received some interest in the Echinades islands at the mouth of the Achelous, also at the expense of the Aetolians.[172] The acquisition of Oeniadae and the other Acarnanian cities, lost since the middle of the third century to Aetolia, had long been a dear ambition of the Acarnanian League. In all probability it had not been slow to bring its desires to the attention of the Romans. One of the arguments used by the Acarnanians to show that they deserved this favor seems to have been the fact that they had not participated in the Trojan War, fought against the ancestors of the Romans. Possibly, too, the Aetolians, getting wind of this, had circulated contemptuous propaganda whose purpose was to show that in the past the Romans had been unable to prevent the Aetolians from holding the cities of Acarnania, nor would they be able to do so on this occasion.[173]

The campaign of 189 had again instructed the Epirotes and the Acarnanians that they must follow Roman behests in international matters. Whatever the merits of the case, both powers evidently considered enemy ambassadors fair game, even when the latters' destination was the power "associated" with the two leagues. Yet both powers were compelled to yield up their victims on peremptory instructions from the Roman authorities. Both powers had had their own reasons for wishing war with Aetolia; nevertheless they must have been aware, too, that Rome expected their co-operation in this respect also. The Epirotes gained nothing from the war except twelve talents; the Acarnanians obtained Oeniadae, although they probably asked for more. Yet they received Oeniadae only, and their acquisition of that city may have been due as much to a Roman desire to demonstrate to the Aetolians that what Rome had given[174] she could take away, as to any wish to please the Acarnanians.

Later generations, like Polybius, would believe that Roman domination of Greece and the world was complete only after the Third Macedonian War in 167. Yet after 189 the belief seems to have been current at Rome, at least in some circles, that Rome's victory over Antiochus was the last important step to world dominion.[175] Hence the need for conciliating the loyalty of Epirus and Acarnania was less urgent than it had been, in the view of the Romans. Thereafter Rome would demand their loyalty as she did that of the Greeks in general.

Chapter IV

THE THIRD MACEDONIAN WAR: DOMINATION

IN THE TWO DECADES following the Syrian (Aetolian) War the Romans showed that whatever might have been their conception of the "liberty" of Greece, its content did not include leaving the Greeks to themselves, to settle their own disputes. In the years following 189 ambassadors and commissioners from Rome journeyed east almost every year to survey, to recommend, and to report; and almost every year embassies from various Greek states, sometimes several at a time, traveled to Rome to lay various petitions before the senate for its decision.[1] Some of the recorded embassies and investigations relate to the area here under consideration.

Many of these embassies were connected with the obvious fact that the senate was not too well disposed either to Philip or to his son and successor, Perseus. The Greek states hoped to take advantage of this Roman prejudice against the Macedonian monarchy to their own profit. Some of the Greek complaints were not unjustified, of course. In the winter of 184/3 a number of Greek ambassadors representing several states, including Epirus, appeared at Rome. Their complaints are not detailed in the sources, but they included claims against Philip for territory, slaves, cattle, and miscellaneous instances of injustice.[2] In response the senate appointed Q. Marcius Philippus to go to Greece to look into the complaints in the summer of 183 B.C.[3]

We do not know exactly what the final decision in these matters was, but since Philip "set aright all things the Romans required of him,"[4] in all probability most, if not all, the claims were settled against him — for he seems seldom to have had the benefit of the doubt from the Roman authorities in this period.[5] Whatever it was the Epirotes wanted, it is quite likely they got it — not from any particular desire to please them, but out of hostility to Philip.

In 180 B.C. occurred the famous embassy of the Achaean Callicrates to Rome. A man noted for his pro-Romanism, he seized the opportunity to advise the senate, in effect, to interfere more extensively and more openly in Greek affairs than in the past. Some Greeks actually thought that laws and treaties and inscribed statutes should take precedence over the wishes of Rome. The senate should make it plain that this was an entirely erroneous view of the situation. Such a decisive action would make it evident that the Greeks were wrong in believing that they could act independently and, the Greeks being impressed by this firm attitude, the pro-Roman parties in Greece would rapidly grow in strength. The particular matter under consideration concerned the treatment of certain Spartan exiles by the Achaeans. The senate had previously made known its wishes in this matter, but without result. The logic of Callicrates' reasoning now impressed the senate so much, however, that it wrote back to Achaea in effect that what Rome as well as the pro-Roman party wanted should be done and that there ought to be more men like Callicrates.[6] Desiring that not only the Achaeans but other Greek states too be not deprived of the benefit of these insights, the senate also informed several other Greek powers of its treatment of Achaea. Among those to whom this communication was sent, the Epirotes and the Acarnanians are expressly mentioned.[7] If there had been any doubt in the minds of the statesmen of the two *koina* concerning what was expected of them, this document should have removed it. All of this, of course, was implicit in the history of Greco-Roman relations for almost two decades; this Roman declaration of policy simply emphasized to the Greeks what that policy was.

As long as a strong Macedonia continued to exist, however, Roman control of Greece was not perfectly assured. And Macedonia had shown surprising resilience in recovery since the Second Macedonian War,[8] while the salutary measures by which Philip had encouraged this recovery continued under Perseus, who came to the throne in 179. Moreover, Perseus showed disturbing signs of a policy which could be interpreted as the resumption of Macedonian interest in the affairs of Greece. His visit to Delphi, for example, could be understood in this light. His reign was marked by a series of incidents which the Romans chose, wilfully or innocently, correctly or incorrectly, to view as proceeding from an anti-Roman bias and as infringements upon the agreements between Philip and Rome.[9] Eumenes, King of Pergamum and enemy of the Antigonids, for his own ends encouraged the Romans to put the worst possible construction on Perseus' acts. One of the most disturbing aspects of Perseus' policy was his encouragement of the debtors, that is to say, the lower classes in Greece. Shortly after his accession he recalled fugitive debtors to Macedonia, and in doing so provided his measure wide publicity in Greece. In Macedonia itself debts to the crown were cancelled.[10] The king was also accused of having interfered in the class struggle in Aetolia on the side of the lower classes.[11] The result was the conciliation to Macedonia of the debtor and lower classes throughout Greece.[12] In turn this must have impelled the upper classes in Greece, generally speaking, to look more and more to Rome as their champion — especially since, being better educated and better informed than the masses, they could form a juster estimate of the overwhelming superiority of Roman power. The same policy of Perseus appeared to Rome as deliberate courting of the anti-Roman faction in Greece. Northwestern Greece could not have remained untouched by these new trends in events; this was perhaps especially true of Epirus, where the socio-economic disorders of the third century continued into the second.[13]

Roman-Macedonian relations, therefore, progressively deteriorated in the course of Perseus' reign and by 172 B.C. the Romans had resolved to reopen hostilities with Macedonia. But in the summer of 172 the Romans were not yet ready to go to war on a large scale and needed time for their preparations. Therefore, in order to gain the necessary interval and to prevent Perseus from consolidating his position in the east while the Roman offensive was getting under way, the senate decided to delude the king into thinking that peace was still possible. Hence in September of 172 it sent to Greece an embassy headed by Q. Marcius Philippus.[14] With it the embassy brought a thousand soldiers to Corcyra. At Corcyra the five envoys divided the soldiers among themselves and decided which states they should severally visit. Marcius himself and A. Atilius were assigned to visit Epirus, Aetolia, and Thessaly, as well as some other places in eastern and southern Greece.[15] From the island Marcius and Atilius crossed to the opposite Epirote mainland where, at the town of Gitana,[16] a short distance from the sea, they appeared before the *concilium* of the Epirotes. The tenor of their remarks has not been preserved, but presumably they rehearsed the grievances which Rome charged against Perseus and intimated that Rome expected Epirote support. Livy says that their speeches were heard with vigorous approval by all present and that the assembly agreed to send a force of four hundred of its young men to protect the Orestae, a tribe which had revolted from Philip during the Second Macedonian War and had been set free by the Romans in compensation. They were neighbors of the Epirotes to the east.[17]

From Epirus the two Romans continued on their way to Aetolia and then to Thessaly. Why they omitted a visit to Acarnania is obscure.[18] Apparently this neglect of the Acarnanians was quite intentional, for there is no mention of Acarnania among the places selected at Corcyra to receive visitations. Perhaps the envoys considered the Acarnanians so intimidated by the Romans that additional prodding was not really necessary. Evidently this neglect worried the Acarnanians, for when the two Romans were in Thessaly a delegation from the Acarnanian *koinon* sought them out. Marcius and Atilius made use of the opportunity to read the Acarnanians a bullying lecture. The Acarnanian envoys were ordered to report at home that their country now had an opportunity to make up for its hostility toward Rome at the time of the wars against Philip and Antiochus (as far as Antiochus was concerned this charge was a gross exaggeration), when it had been "deceived by royal promises." When undeserving the Acarnanians had had trial of the clemency of Rome; they should try to merit Roman generosity in the future.[19]

Having thus delivered themselves of these smug and lofty sentiments, the Roman envoys continued on their way to the Vale of Tempe, where they conferred with Perseus. The king was induced to send an embassy to Rome, a truce being granted for the purpose.[20] The Macedonians of course accomplished nothing at Rome and were harshly dismissed (winter, 171).[21] In midwinter 172/1 war on Macedonia was formally declared at Rome,[22] and the consul for 171, P. Licinius Crassus, received Macedonia as his province.[23]

Even while the Roman envoys had been in Greece, in November, 172, the praetor, Cn. Sicinius, crossed to Apollonia to garrison the coastal cities in Illyria so as to provide a safe port of debarkation for the Roman army the following spring.[24] During the succeeding winter Sicinius was ordered to send to A. Atilius in Thessaly two thousand men to secure Larisa.[25] Almost certainly this force must have passed through Epirus to get there, since the direct Pindus route was obviously impossible. As far as we know, the march was without incident. Nevertheless, in the spring of the next year the consul, Crassus, having landed at Apollonia, evidently did not march by the most direct way through Epirus to Thessaly (*i.e.,* via Atintania, Parauaea, and Tymphaea — along the Aous valley). Instead, his route lay through the heart of Epirus, for he crossed into Thessaly by way of Athamania.[26] It had been suggested[27] with great plausibility, in view of the sequel, that one of the reasons for this detour was to impress the Epirotes with the spectacle of a Roman army in full panoply. There must have been some particular reason for choosing this route, for the terrain was much more difficult than that of the Aous valley.[28] During the course of the indecisive campaign against Perseus that followed, Crassus may have had some suspicion that the loyalty of Ambracia was not all it should have been, for he sent Q. Mucius, one of his legates, with two thousand men to pass the winter there.[29] For Roman communications and supply lines to eastern Greece the city was of vital importance, of course.[30]

In 170, however, Roman communications between the Adriatic and eastern Greece were seriously impaired by the defection of a considerable part of Epirus. That country had played, as we have seen, a singularly unheroic part in the struggles that had transpired in Greece since the conclusion of the Social War in 217. At all costs the Epirotes had attempted to remain as untouched as possible by the wars that had occurred in Greece during the intervening period. In the earliest years of Roman intervention in the Balkans Epirus had at first been ignored and then treated with leniency by the Roman government. With the conclusion of the Syrian War, or even before, this policy of leniency had ceased. Rome had seen fit to interfere regularly in the affairs of Greece, and that she did not consider the Epirotes any less subject to her hegemony than any other Greek state she had explicitly declared to the Epirote government in 180. And there was in Epirus a party ready and willing to give heed to Rome's declaration that her wishes were to be considered sovereign.[31] Whatever his backsliding in 192/1, Charops seems to have been firmly convinced thereafter that Rome had intervened in the Balkans with every intention of making her stay there permanent. This elder Charops had a son named Machatas who died before his father, leaving a son of his own named for his grandfather—the younger Charops. Undoubtedly in order to please Roman vanity and to smooth the way for his grandson and his family in future dealings with Rome, after the death of Machatas the elder Charops had sent the younger to Rome to learn to read and speak the Latin tongue. This was a step probably almost unique in Greco-Roman relations at this juncture. Shortly after the younger Charops returned from Rome, the elder died, and the grandson, although still little more than a boy, attempted to assume the grandfather's position of authority in Epirote politics. His policy was extreme pro-Romanism, a policy which the elder Charops had perhaps already laid down as the proper course to follow. If so, the younger man probably pursued his objective with more headstrong rashness than the crafty opportunism of the elder statesman had envisioned. There were also, as one would expect, other Epirote politicians who urged subservience to Rome; a certain Nicias[32] and perhaps a man named Nestor[33] are known to us by name. The chronology of these events cannot be determined, but Polybius[34] seems to imply that the younger Charops began his attempt to play a leading role in Epirote affairs within the few years just before the outbreak of the Third Macedonian War.

The principal Epirote statesmen after the death of the elder Charops—Antinous, Cephalus, and Theodotus[35]—at first paid little attention to the urgings of the stripling. In view of the famous senate letter of 180, and the character of Charops, it is possible he issued threats and warnings as well. Cephalus, probably the guiding spirit[36] of the three statesmen, seems to have remained unimpressed with the senate's pronunciamento and to have desired to pursue the policy of peace and neutrality hitherto followed by the state and probably advocated by the elder Charops himself until the last period of his life. Accordingly Cephalus and his party had first hoped that war would be avoided, and after it broke out aspired to a course which took due regard for Epirus' association with Rome, but which also maintained the sovereignty of the state.[37] But the war's outbreak gave a new turn to affairs. At once Charops began to calumniate his political rivals to the Romans, by half-truths and distortions representing the actions of the moderate party as in reality being pro-Macedonian. If any credence at all can be placed in his charges, Cephalus and his fellows seem in the past to have enjoyed some special relationship to the Antigonid monarchy. Possibly these charges merely boil down to acts which were intended to make Epirus the friend of Macedonia as well as of Rome. We can easily imagine Charops making the short journey to Apollonia, or the shorter one to Corcyra, to lay these charges before the Romans in the winter of 172/1 and afterward. Crassus' march through Epirus in 171 may well have been the result of such representations.

Yet in 172 when Marcius and Atilius appeared before the *concilium* of the Epirotes at Gitana, their speeches against Perseus had been very well received, according to Livy.[38] There is of course the possibility that Livy has exaggerated the welcome reception given the Roman envoys. Another consideration, however, also suggests itself. Interesting particularly to Americans is the role which regionalism, or tribalism, still played in Epirote politics. The three opponents of Charops were all Molossians, and Cephalus had held high office in the local government of Molossis.[39] With some additions, most of the Epirotes who joined Perseus in 170 were Molossians. But in 172 the *concilium* of the Epirotes had been held at Gitana, ten miles from the coast. The exact site of this city is now unknown, but it must have been located in the territories of one of the two great coastal tribes, Chaonians or Thesprotians. Gitana was therefore easy of access to these two tribes, either by sea along the coast, or by land along the valleys of Epirus which run parallel to the coast for the most part. On the other hand it was not nearly so easy of access to the Molossians of the interior, separated from the coast by several chains of difficult and contorted mountains. Now the summoning of the *concilium* to Gitana, rather than to Phoenice, the league capital, suggests at once that the meeting was not a regular one, that it was a special one summoned to hear the Roman ambassadors at their convenience and probably at relatively short notice. Hence it is likely that the Molossians were poorly represented at Gitana, if at all. If this conclusion be correct, the *concilium* represented not all Epirus, really, but rather those parts of it which tended more to subservience to Rome and which were therefore inclined to follow the leadership of Charops to avoid trouble.

Had Cephalus and his party been better represented at Gitana, probably a much less enthusiastic answer would have been returned to the Roman envoys than was actually the case. But by 170 it was becoming apparent to Cephalus that his own position and his party's was growing more and more impossible. Before his eyes was the fate of leaders of the party similar to his own in Aetolia. Three members of the moderate party there had arbitrarily been seized and carried off to Rome as a result of charges fabricated against them by Lyciscus, the Charops of Aetolia. Hence, reluctantly, Cephalus determined to support Perseus. It is easy to see why Perseus rather than Rome. Cephalus and his followers were already compromised in Roman eyes, thanks to Charops; joining Rome would mean political eclipse by Charops, the proved friend of the Romans; on a more idealistic plane, finally, adherence to the Roman cause would definitely confirm Epirus in her subjection to Roman hegemony. It is apparent that Polybius sympathizes with Cephalus and his friends. The historian describes the man as wise and stable,[40] and his policy as noble and principled.[41] The reason is not far to seek: Cephalus' policy was essentially that pursued in Achaea by Philopoemen and by Lycortas, Polybius' father. Nevertheless, the course chosen by Cephalus and his associates was unwise and ill-considered. If there ever had been a day when a third-rate power like Epirus could profitably have joined an enemy of Rome to maintain its independence, that day was long past with the first two Macedonian Wars. For only a fraction of the Epirotes to revolt was merely to invite whatever reprisals the senate might choose to inflict, with little or no chance of success to justify that risk.

Other reasons for the revolt of the Molossians (rather than of the Thesprotians, or Chaonians, or Epirus as a whole) may only be suggested in view of the lack of evidence in our sources. The Molossians had once been the ruling people in Epirus in the days of the monarchy. Perhaps under the present government they resented the fact that their tribe had lost that dominant position; that Phoenice, the capital, was in Chaonia. True, under Pyrrhus and his successors the seat of government had been located not in Molossis but at Ambracia, but a Molossian king had reigned there.[42] In 170 patriotic Molossian pride might well recall the days, then a century past, when the Epirotes under a Molossian king had all but conquered the Romans on their own ground. Finally, one can only suggest that Molossis, locked in the interior of Epirus, was perhaps economically the poorest region of the country,[43] and that social grievances might have been stronger there than elsewhere, predisposing the people to favor Perseus, the debtors' friend.

Evidently unaware that matters were about to come to a head in Epirus, the consul for 170, A. Hostilius Mancinus, arrived in the east in the spring of that year.[44] On his way through Epirus to assume command of the Roman army, Mancinus arrived at Phanote, a city in Chaonia, where he stayed at the house of a certain Nestor, possibly a man from an obscure town in Epirus named Oropus.[45] Theodotus and Philostratus, the latter also possibly a Molossian, conceived the bold plan of kidnapping the Roman general and handing him over to Perseus. Probably the plot had been laid before the arrival of the consul, who was almost certain to pass through Epirus. Otherwise Perseus might not have had time to receive the letters telling him of the arrival of the Roman, to verify their authenticity and good faith, and to arrive in Epirus in time. The alternative assumption is that Mancinus delayed for some reason in Epirus and no reason for such a delay is evident. It could not have been that he was aware of unrest among the Epirotes and wanted to remedy it; if so, he would have come with a force of some size, and his subsequent flight leaves the strong impression that he probably had only a small retinue.

In any event, now that Mancinus was in Epirus, Theodotus and Philostratus kept sending messages to Perseus urging him to come and grasp his prey. The king hastened to comply with their exhortations, but was unexpectedly held up by the Molossians, who had occupied the bridge over the Aous by which the king had expected to cross. Almost too late Nestor, probably a member of the extreme pro-Roman party, came to suspect that something was amiss. He may have heard disquieting rumors of Perseus' advance from people living in the hill country between Phanote and the Aous.[46] Warning his guest, Nestor hurried the consul away from Phanote by night to Gitana. There the consul renounced his design of traveling by land through Epirus and took ship for the east.

The foregoing account obviously poses a difficulty. Since the Molossians[47] opposed the passage of Perseus over the Aous, they were not yet on Perseus' side in the spring of 170. Yet Cephalus, the chief Molossian leader, is said to have resolved, regretfully, on a policy of resistance to Rome when he heard that three moderate Aetolian leaders had been deported to Rome on the false charges of the pro-Roman Lyciscus, "after the cavalry battle."[48] This probably refers to a Roman clash with Perseus in late summer, 171, in which large numbers of horse were engaged.[49] The deportation of the three Aetolians, Polybius implies, took place soon thereafter and news of this must have reached Epirus very quickly, by late autumn at the latest. Yet the Molossians have not yet gone over to the side of Perseus the following spring. Evidently Cephalus was quite slow in making up his mind to resort to open defiance of Rome, as Polybius implies elsewhere.[50] It is noteworthy that, although Cephalus is considered the leading Molossian statesman and although the rebellion of Molossis is credited to him,[51] he is not mentioned in connection with the plot of Theodotus and Philostratus. As a matter of fact the latter two are called by Diodorus,[52] whose source was probably Polybius, the most ardent of the pro-Macedonians. Furthermore Theodotus and Philostratus acted on their own initative,[53] and their part in the conspiracy seems to have been merely that of informing Perseus when the time was right and urging him to act with speed. It is not impossible that Theodotus and Philostratus desired to manufacture an incident which would force Cephalus into open revolt, and possibly one which would compromise the whole Epirote *koinon*.

At any rate, the Molossians had revolted before midwinter 170/69[54] under the leadership of Cephalus, and probably sometime, therefore, in the last eight months of 170. Even though it had failed, the conspiracy of Theodotus and Philostratus very possibly induced Cephalus to see that there could be no accommodation between Rome and his party in the future. If so, the Molossian revolt may be dated to midsummer, 170. Perseus seems to have sent a force to Epirus to look after his interests there in 170. It was quartered the following winter at Phanote.[55] Some other parts of Epirus revolted too,[56] including Phanote in Chaonia.[57] Possibly the city feared Roman retribution for the attempt to kidnap Mancinus. Tymphaea, which secured the communications of Molossis with Perseus, also probably revolted.[58]. The loss of even this part[59] of Epirus to the Roman cause was of a considerable importance, for the Romans had thus lost control of their most direct line of communications to their bases in Illyria, Corcyra, and the Ionian Islands.[60]

With part of Epirus disaffected it became even more necessary to secure the loyalty of Acarnania. Accordingly, in the autumn of 170[61] an embassy composed of C. Popilius and Cn. Octavius, bearing a decree of the senate that no aid was to be furnished Roman magistrates save by its express instructions, was sent by Mancinus not only to the Peloponnese and Aetolia, but to Acarnania as well.[62] Here also the envoys presumably published the contents of the senate's order, although there is no statement to that effect in the sources. Evidently the senate was desirous of conciliating the Greeks who had been outraged by the unconscionable and unethical conduct of Roman officials in Greece during the war. In Acarnania the Roman envoys appeared before an assembly at Thyrrheum, where the leaders of the pro-Roman party, Aeschrion, Glaucus, and Chremas, asked the Romans to put garrisons in Acarnania, alleging that the pro-Macedonian party was wooing the people away from Rome. The moderate leader, Diogenes, opposed this suggestion on the ground that the Acarnanians had done nothing to justify such a Roman action. Probably with considerable justice he added that the native advocates of such a procedure were primarily looking for a means to establish their own ascendancy in Acarnania. Most of the assembly assented to the views of Diogenes. Inasmuch as the envoys had orders from the senate,[63] if not from Mancinus as well, to conciliate the Greeks they allowed themselves to be swayed by the arguments of Diogenes. Thanking the Acarnanians, the Romans departed to rejoin Mancinus. The restraint and the conciliatory spirit of the Romans on this occasion are surprising. The senate had realized the dangers of too heavy-handed a policy in Greece while a war was in progress in the peninsula—even if many of its field commanders had not. It must have been tempting to garrison the cities of Acarnania and thus insure the Roman lines of communication into the Ambracian Gulf. On the other hand, such a measure, in view of the distaste of most Acarnanians for it, might well provoke Acarnania to follow the example of Molossis (assuming, as is probable, that the revolt of Cephalus had already occurred). This would defeat the chief Roman object in Acarnania, to keep Roman lines of communication open, and might well require the presence of Roman troops to put down the "rebellion" at a time when they would be better deployed directly against Perseus. Lastly, the garrisoning of a friendly state might have the worst possible effect in Greece at large. It may be, therefore, that the Roman government was attempting a temporary return to the policy of conciliation in these regions of northwestern Greece, a policy openly abandoned since 180. To make doubly sure, however, after Popilius and Octavius had made their report to Mancinus, the consul sent the former with a thousand men to garrison Ambracia during the winter.[64] Here Popilius could not only guard this key point on Roman communications and supply lines, but also keep an eye on the activities of the Epirotes to the north and the Acarnanians to the south.[65]

Perseus waited until the snows of winter could guard the passes of the Thessalian mountains for him before he ventured to take advantage of his opportunities in the west of the peninsula—where in Illyria King Genthius was ill-disposed toward Rome, and where Molossis had already revolted.[66] The king thereupon embarked upon a fairly successful campaign in Illyria. During the same winter a Roman officer, App. Claudius,[67] attacked Phanote in Epirus, a town held at this time by a strong Macedonian garrison commanded by a certain Clevas. Serving with the Roman troops were some six thousand auxiliaries from Thesprotis and Chaonia.[68] Evidently these two principal Epirote tribes were actively co-operating with the Romans at this juncture. Despite this local assistance Claudius' attempts to take the place failed completely.[69]

Meanwhile, at the suggestion of the Epirotes (*i.e.*, the Molossians and the other revolted Epirotes),[70] Perseus marched from Elimea in Macedonia to the Aetolian city of Stratus.[71] An attempt to put the city into his hands by treachery was foiled by the timely arrival of Popilius with a Roman force from Ambracia. The Roman commander had been warned just in time by the pro-Roman party in Stratus.[72] The Epirote "deserters," as Livy calls them, and the leader of the pro-Macedonian faction in Stratus were unable to persuade the king to persevere in his plan to take Stratus after surprise had failed.[73] The Romans had in fact narrowly averted a grave disaster. Had Perseus succeeded in his attempt, possibly all Aetolia, Acarnania, and Epirus might have joined his cause.[74]

The report of the king's march on Stratus, however, intimidated Claudius into raising the siege of Phanote. Clevas followed with his forces and inflicted considerable losses on the retreating Roman force as it passed through a defile of the mountains. The Macedonian commander was joined by an Epirote force under Philostratus, and the combined forces advanced into Atintania where they lured the Epirote garrison of Antigoneia from behind the city walls and inflicted severe losses on it. Claudius, realizing that a virtual stalemate had been reached for the time being, dismissed his Epirote auxiliaries and returned to Illyria.[75] Claudius' attempt to deal with Clevas and to commence the reduction of the revolted districts of Epirus and reopen the Epirote route to Thessaly had failed.[76]

Shortly after these events, in early spring, 169, the consul, Q. Marcius Philippus, arrived in Thessaly, via Corcyra, Actium in Acarnania, and Ambracia, thus using the southern route since the northern, through Epirus, was closed.[77] His choice of route clearly shows the strategic importance of Acarnania, as does the journey of C. Marcius Figulus, praetor for the fleet, who accompanied his chief as far as Actium, then rounded Leucas and sailed into the Corinthian Gulf.[78]

Little of importance happened in the west in 169. Claudius requested the Achaeans to send him five thousand men to aid in reducing the Molossians. The consul Marcius, hearing of the request, sent the historian Polybius, who was with him in Thessaly, to Achaea in order to see that the request was refused.[79] Polybius managed to have the request turned down on the ground that there was no authorization for it from the senate, in accordance with the decree of that body issued the year before.[80] The Roman army also purchased a large amount of grain in Epirus during the year,[81] undoubtedly in Chaonia and Thesprotis.

The war had now dragged on for three campaigns with virtually no progress toward a decision made on either side. In 168, however, the new consul, L. Aemilius Paulus, brought both the war and the Antigonid monarchy to an end by the decisive victory of Pydna, fought June 22.[82] With similar dispatch the praetor L. Anicius brought the war in Illyria to a close by defeating Genthius, who had finally been persuaded by Perseus' bribes to enter the war on the Macedonian side.

Having thus reduced Illyria to obedience to the Roman will, Anicius marched south into Epirus. Phanote was his first objective, and as he approached the town the inhabitants marched out to surrender, wearing the fillets of suppliants on their heads. From Phanote the praetor marched into Molossis, all of whose cities surrendered at once—with four exceptions. At Passaro, Antinous and Theodotus restrained the citizens from surrendering; but when the Roman army actually appeared before the city walls, the two statesmen were unable to control the apprehensions of the people. Since the multitude were bent on opening the gates, the two men ran out and committed suicide by hurling themselves upon the advance guard of the Romans. The people of Tecmo seem to have put Cephalus, who had taken refuge there, to death and then surrendered to the Romans. The two remaining towns capitulated soon thereafter. Thus all Molossis was reduced to submission, probably in autumn, 168, since Anicius immediately afterward disposed his troops in strategic places to pass the winter and returned to Illyria.[83] The rapidity of the Roman pacification and the alacrity with which all the "revolted" towns surrendered also suggests that the battle of Pydna had already been fought and that the Epirote cantons were the last remaining belligerents. Accordingly the whole campaign may have occupied August and September, 168.

With the victory of the Romans over Perseus and his allies, everywhere in Greece the pro-Roman parties thrust themselves eagerly and aggressively to the fore at home, while their leaders traveled joyously to the Roman camp in Macedonia to bask in Roman favor and to calumniate their political opponents in the several Greek states before Paulus and the senatorial commission of ten which had been sent to assist the general in regulating the affairs of Macedonia. Among the scalawags who came to congratulate Paulus and prepare the downfall of their foes at home were Charops and Nicias from Epirus and Chremas from Acarnania.[84] They assured the Romans that not only had the openly pro-Macedonian party favored the cause of Perseus, but a large party in the various states had worked secretly to hinder the Roman success. They were, of course, describing the moderate parties in the most disparaging light possible. The names of these men, doubtless including all of the opposition leaders, they gladly furnished the Roman authorities. Paulus and the ten sent letters to the *strategoi* of Acarnania, Epirus, and the other states, demanding that these persons be sent to Rome to plead their cases, only those individuals most eminent for their services being excepted.[85] It is possible that Paulus may not have approved of the proceedings personally.[86] These persons thus summoned to Rome were to be detained in Italy for fifteen years. There was some precedent for it; the Romans had kept adherents of Demetrius of Pharos under arrest in their dominions for some years after 219.[87]

The ten senatorial commissioners who joined Paulus bore with them a *senatusconsultum* ordaining the general lines for a settlement of Macedonian affairs.[88] The Antigonid monarchy was abolished and Macedonia divided into four regions with separate governments. Atintania and Tymphaea, however, were included in Macedonia IV, the westernmost of the four regions.[89] Atintania had been part of the Roman "protectorate" since the Second Macedonian War,[90] but Tymphaea was part of Epirus.[91] It is quite likely that it had joined the Molossians when they had "revolted" to Perseus in 170.[92] Moreover, Parauaea, the valley of the upper Aous, was almost certainly added to Macedonia IV, and this was Epirote territory too.[93]

This transfer of territory from Epirus to Macedonia IV is probably to be considered part of the punishment meted out to Epirus for the defection of part of the *koinon* in the war, but the addition of Atintania to these territories shows that the principal motive must have been something else. One is at once struck by the fact that virtually the whole Aous valley, the most direct route to Thessaly and Macedonia other than the track over Pindus, is involved. The Romans had taken elaborate precautions to weaken Macedonia. It seems, therefore, that they regarded this route as safer in the hands of a quarter of Macedonia than in the control of the Epirote *koinon*. During the war they had been seriously inconvenienced when this route had been closed to them. For the future they were guaranteeing in this fashion that it should not be closed.

Acarnania also did not escape without loss of territory on this occasion. The island of Leucas with the city of the same name, the capital of the league, was taken from the league by the ten commissioners.[94] It was probably erected into a "free" city[95] with a status probably resembling that of Corcyra (since 229) and the other autonomous islands and cities of the Adriatic coast. No reason for this treatment of Acarnania is specified or even implied. There is no hint that that state had acted disloyally during the war, as had part of Epirus. In all probability the Romans wished to weaken Acarnania, which was in a position to harm their eastern communications, as well as to detach Leucas, like the other important stepping-stones to the east — Zacynthus, Cephallenia, Corcyra — from dependence on any other power and make it "independent," *i.e.*, subject only to Roman hegemony. Finally, as a gesture of her authority, as in the similar case of the Aetolians and Oeniadae in 189, what Rome had given (in 197/6), Rome could take away. This would serve as a salutary lesson to others who had benefited by Roman favors, and remind them that the principle of obedience to Rome enunciated in 180 was again in effect. Acarnania, which had displayed some signs of independence during the war, was to be reminded of the real meaning of Roman *amicitia*. With the nearest great power from whom Rome stood in any conceivable danger as far away as the Taurus range, the senate could afford to take off the velvet gloves in all parts of Greece.

In the autumn of 168 L. Anicius had returned from Epirus to Illyria to meet with the five commissioners sent out by the senate to regulate the affairs of Illyria.[96] Illyria having been given a settlement similar to that of Macedonia, Anicius returned to winter quarters at Passaro in Epirus.[97] Apparently, according to Livy's description of the activities of the Illyrian commission,[98] it had no instructions regarding Epirus; since territory had been taken from Epirus by the Macedonian commission of ten, Epirote affairs must have fallen in the competence of the latter commission. The Epirote League as a whole had been punished for the defection of an important section of its members by the loss of considerable territory; but those who had actually revolted, the Molossians and some others, were still apparently in the status of *dediticii*, into which they had entered when they had surrendered to Anicius.[99] As *dediticii* they were legally at the absolute disposal of the Romans, to be treated in whatsoever fashion the latter wished.[100] Even if the Molossians comprehended the full meaning of *deditio*, nevertheless, judging from past examples of its working in Greece, they might well suppose that their treatment would not be excessively severe.

Probably in the spring of 167, having finished arranging the affairs of Macedonia, Paulus commenced his homeward march with his army. Half of his troops were dispatched to Illyria to ravage the lands of those Illyrians who had helped Perseus in the war.[101] Paulus himself marched to Passaro in Molossis and encamped there.

Thence he sent a message to the near-by camp of Anicius that the latter should not be disturbed at what was about to happen. The senate had granted to the soldiers the plunder of the communities of Molossis and some others that had "revolted" to Perseus. Paulus then sent centurions to the various places concerned, with instructions to inform the people that they had come to withdraw the Roman garrisons so that Epirus might be "free." Thereafter ten of the leading men of each community were commanded to appear before the Roman general. These notables were instructed that all the gold and silver was to be put out in the streets. The soldiers were divided up and assigned by cohorts to the various places involved, their marches being carefully timed so that each cohort would arrive at its destination at the proper moment. On the appointed day the treasure was first collected, then about ten o'clock in the morning the soldiers were loosed to pillage. In this way some seventy communities were plundered (obviously they could not all have been cities), and if the figure of Livy may be trusted, some 150,000 persons carried off into slavery. After the walls of these cities and villages had been thrown down, Paulus collected his troops and marched to Illyria, undoubtedly leaving the Epirotes "free" behind him.[102] As is obvious, the whole operation had been conducted with the greatest of that military efficiency and celerity for which the Roman army was so justly renowned, and with cautious foresight and detailed planning.

From Illyria Paulus sailed to Italy with his victorious army. Shortly thereafter Anicius followed him. But before the latter departed, he summoned a meeting attended by the "other Epirotes," that is, those who had not been punished in the manner described above, and by the Acarnanians. Those who attended were told that certain persons of each *koinon* were ordered to go to Italy to appear before the senate.[103] Still others seem to have been executed.[104] The meaning of this action is not clear. Paulus and the ten commissioners for Greece had already written to the *strategoi* of the various *koina*, including Epirus and Acarnania, to list the men who must go to Rome for trial.[105] Possibly on this occasion Anicius reiterated the list already sent to Epirus and Acarnania, but this seems unlikely; after what had just been done to Molossis, the Romans could be sure that their commands would be obeyed with fear and trembling. Hence this must be a supplementary list addressed to these states only. Either the Romans had learned of other "enemies" in some unrecorded fashion, or, more likely, Charops and Chremas and their friends, in their zeal to be of service, had thoughtfully provided a second list.

The treatment of these persons, of course, is mild indeed compared to the ferocious punishment inflicted upon the Molossians. It is quite clear that the proceedings in Molossis were undertaken by Paulus, not on his own initiative, but on instructions from the senate.[106] The punishment, therefore, was official state policy. Inasmuch as no extant source assigns any particular motive for these drastic reprisals, various suggestions and conjectures have been advanced by modern scholars to explain them. It has been thought that a desire for revenge for Pyrrhus' invasion of Italy was the cause. But this plainly will not do. Isolated events are not avenged a century later. Pyrrhus had been a Molossian, true, but he had been king of Epirus; hence all of Epirus should have been ravaged if this were the motive. Yet only a part of Epirus was punished. Again, it has been suggested[107] that the Epirotes had committed some unrecorded act of treachery for which the punishment visited upon them in 167 was requital. But Plutarch would certainly have mentioned such an act, if there had been one, the better to exonerate his hero, Aemilius Paulus.[108] H. H. Scullard[109] has recently advanced an interesting theory that the punishment was suggested to the Romans by Charops, and that when Polybius remarks,[110] "To such a degree was their [*i.e.*, the Epirotes'] leader less god-fearing and more contemptuous of the laws than others. For I think that neither has there been nor will there be a man more ferocious or crooked than Charops," he is thinking of Charops as the instigator of the Roman destruction of Molossis. Charops, taking advantage of his many friendships at Rome,[111] probably among the unprincipled men who were coming to the fore in the senate by 167, was able to induce the senate to decree the devastation of the lands of his political enemies. The only certain points are, however, that Charops was considered by Polybius to be the worst of the quislings, and that Charops had many friends at Rome.[112]

In any event, it seems certain that the punishment of the revolted Epirotes was out of all proportion to their offense. The Romans had long treated the Epirotes with especial consideration, beginning with the First Macedonian War. Epirote tergiversation in the Syrian War had been forgiven. Now part of the league had reciprocated this treatment by going over to Perseus. This "desertion" was particularly exasperating, since the territories involved controlled one of Rome's most important routes to the east. Likewise the defection of some of the Illyrians had the effect of posing an additional threat to those same communications. Hence the territories of the peoples concerned in both cases were devastated with Roman thoroughnesss. The punishment was vastly more severe than the crime, at least in Epirus; but men like M. Popilius who attacked the harmless Ligurians, or Cassius Longinus who was proud of similar exploits in the Alps, or the praetor Lucretius who had made an evil name for himself in the war in Greece by double-dealing, stealing, and plundering, or Q. Marcius Philippus who had treacherously lied to Perseus about the possibility of peace in 172[113] — such men would not boggle at that. The conciliatory policy in Epirus and Acarnania had produced in neither case the instant subservience to Roman will which the senate had come to expect. Acarnania lost Leucas for not eagerly accepting the privilege of a Roman garrison; Epirus lost territory and had about a third of her remaining possessions turned into a desert because one of her tribes went over to Perseus. In neither case did the offenses merit the punishment; the disproportion of the punishment to the offense was roughly similar in the two cases. The dullest of the Greeks in Epirus and Acarnania and elsewhere now knew the meaning of *libertas*.[114]

Greece did not become a province, in the sense of a region having a Roman supervisor permanently in residence, until the reign of Augustus.[115] But in virtually every other sense of the word "province"[116] Greece was a part of the *imperium Romanum* after 167 B.C., as indeed she probably had been from the Roman point of view for a long time before. The sources for the period after that year are poor: Livy is reduced to an epitome, and only scattered fragments of Polybius survive; Pausanias gives some dubious assistance.

After 167 the *koinon* of the Epirotes continued to exist, with its seat at Phoenice as before.[117] Economic and social distress seems to have continued as before, at least for a time;[118] perhaps some indication of this is to be seen in the virtual cessation of the Epirote coinage after 167.[119] Certainly Molossis had been ruined, and probably Phanote and its territory, as well as other places. In these troubled waters fished Charops, bolstered by having been the chief of the pro-Roman party in the war, and without serious opposition—since the executions and deportations of 167 had shown that to cross him was virtual suicide. Polybius[120] calls him the most evil man of his day. Not only was he an arch-quisling; he was completely devoid of all principle, a gangster. With his associates—his friends Myrton and Nicanor, father and son, and his own mother, Philotis, who was in charge of terrorizing women —Charops proceeded to inaugurate a reign of crime and terror. Some citizens were openly murdered, others secretly assassinated, still others driven into exile; the property of all of these was confiscated, undoubtedly to the profit of Charops and his henchmen. The assembly at Phoenice legalized his acts, bribed by the tyrant or terror-stricken at the fate of those who offered resistance.[121] That the Romans, however, sanctioned toadies, but not criminals, as their agents in Greece, was made apparent when shortly before 160[122] Charops went to Rome, where probably those he had exiled[123] had been spreading tales about him. Despite the fact that he had come prepared with large sums of money for bribery,[124] he failed to obtain sanction for his acts, and some of the senators, including Paulus himself, refused to see him. The senate announced it would send envoys to investigate, but Charops gave out that the answer of the Romans was favorable, presumably when he reached home again.[125] Unfortunately we know nothing of what this commission did in Epirus, but it probably issued an unfavorable report. At any rate, some time later, perhaps in 158 or 157, Charops died at Brundisium,[126] whether in exile, or on his way to or from Rome seeking the senate's favor again.[127] The troubles of Epirus, however, were unfortunately not over as yet. Some sort of disagreement broke out between two groups, one holding Phoenice, and one exiled (those exiled by Charops?). Each side sent an embassy to Rome. The senate replied it would instruct the embassy it was about to send to Illyria to investigate the situation in Epirus as well.[128] The outcome is unknown. During all this period the Epirotes deported in 167, together with their fellows from Acarnania and other parts of Greece, were pining away in Italy. About 165 the news that the senate refused to release these men, as an Achaean embassy had requested, was a source of great joy to Charops and other of his ilk throughout Greece.[129] Finally in 151 the remaining exiles, the Achaeans and the others,[130] were restored to their homes.[131]

In Acarnania also the *koinon* continued[132] with its capital now at Thyrrheum,[133] which thereafter minted the league coins.[134] The league may even have undertaken some sort of diplomatic relations with Macedonia.[135] Although we have no direct evidence of Roman regulation here, there can be no doubt that the *koinon* was governed in the Roman interest, and his own, by Chremas, its chief pro-Roman leader during the Third Macedonian War. Chremas died apparently about the same time as Charops, and Polybius tells us that conditions improved considerably thereafter.[136]

Thus Rome continued to govern Epirus and Acarnania, like the rest of Greece, through pro-Roman parties and through embassies and letters passing between Italy and Greece from both sides; while after 148, of course, the governor of Macedonia, which was made a formal province in that year,[137] could act as general agent-in-charge of Greece as well. Roman, or at least Italian, settlers began to appear in larger numbers in Greece, including the northwestern portions of the country.[138] Even if a history of Epirus and Acarnania could be written to cover the period following 167— and certainly that after 146—it would be merely local, provincial history.

By the end of the Third Macedonian War, then, Roman control was irrevocably fastened upon Greece. The Achaean War and the Fourth Macedonian War much more nearly resemble revolts against an established hegemony of Rome than wars of one independent power against another. The policy of Rome which had eventually achieved this result had followed a path in Epirus and Acarnania which differed somewhat from that followed elsewhere in Greece, but the end result was the same. In the beginning, during the First Illyrian War and immediately afterward, the Roman government had not embarked upon a program of extending its hegemony in the east beyond what it considered essential to preserve order. Rome had studiously ignored the Epirote and Acarnanian Leagues to the south of her new "protectorate." This is the more striking since it would have been only natural to expect that Rome, had she had any real interests in Greece at that time, would have made some move toward clearing up her ambiguous relationship with the two leagues which had been allied to the Illyrians. Nevertheless she did not do so, even after the Second Illyrian War, although these two states had in the meanwhile become closely tied to Macedonia, the power which must obviously be the most concerned at Roman possession of a trans-Adriatic "protectorate."

With the outbreak of the First Macedonian War in 215 Rome entered into a technical relationship of hostility with Epirus and Acarnania, allies of Macedonia. In the case of Acarnania this technical state of war was transformed into an actual one with the Aetolian-Roman accord in 211, but Epirus seems to have reached an informal arrangement with both the Romans and Philip which permitted her to remain neutral. After the Peace of Phoenice in 205, both Epirus and Acarnania entered into a state of technical informal *amicitia* or *societas* with Rome, inasmuch as the two northwestern Greek powers, being included in the Peace of Phoenice, had participated in nonhostile relations with Rome.

During the course of the First Macedonian War the Romans had become interested in the possibilities of eastward expansion of their influence. Accordingly Epirus and Acarnania assumed an importance to Rome out of proportion to their actual worth, because of their strategic position which dominated the best land and sea routes to Greece and the Hellenistic Orient beyond. In the Second Macedonian War, therefore, the Romans treated Epirus with especial deference when marching across Epirote territory. Acarnania, however, sided with Macedonia in the war, particularly since the Romans had associated themselves once again with the Aetolians, ancient enemies of the Acarnanians, who still held several Acarnanian cities. The Romans attempted to win over Acarnania by a combination of persuasion and trickery, but were finally compelled to use force, and captured Leucas. After the war, however, the island was returned to the league promptly. While Flamininus interfered with many of the Greek states after the war, both by drawing boundaries and by regulating their internal concerns, Epirus and even Acarnania were treated with the utmost solicitude as belonging to the most-favored class of Greek states, such as Attica.

This policy of conciliation probably did not produce important results in either of the two states, which in all likelihood continued to regard the Romans as intrusive barbarians. Their allegiance was probably held primarily through fear, as the Epirotes demonstrated when they tried to be friends to both sides during the war with Antiochus. Acarnania, however, adhered to the Roman cause, but one suspects that this was as much owing to her aversion to the Aetolian allies of Antiochus and her fear of the Roman fleet as anything else. Nevertheless, Acarnania was given Oeniadae, one of her cities which had been held by the Aetolians with but a brief interruption (219/11) since the middle of the third century. The Epirotes, however, had been given to understand that friendship with Rome meant unswerving allegiance to Roman foreign policy.

In 180 the senate in effect informed both leagues that the practice of deferring to Rome should be followed in any matter in which the Roman government evinced an interest, when the senate made clear to the two leagues as well as to Achaea and other Greek states that its wishes were to be followed at all costs. Nevertheless, in Epirus and Acarnania a neutral party, which rejected this humiliating subservience to Rome, continued to command considerable adherence. During the Third Macedonian War this party in Epirus was driven by the pro-Roman faction there, led by the younger Charops — a man distinguished even among his fellow toadies and quislings for villainy — into open revolt against Rome. Since regionalism was still an important political force in Epirus, and since the Epirote moderate party had its principal strength in Molossis, it was the Molossians, along with citizens of a few other places, that revolted. Because of this revolt Epirus, after the Roman victory, lost to the nearest of the four states into which Macedonia was divided by the Romans those portions of Epirote territory which controlled the most important land route to the east. But the parts of the Epirote *koinon* that had actually been in revolt were with systematic thoroughness transformed by the Romans into a desert, as a lesson to Epirus and to the rest of the Greeks. With the Antigonid monarchy gone, the Seleucid Empire pushed beyond Taurus and turning its interest to the farther east, and with the Ptolemaic kingdom sinking into the position of a client-state dependent on

Rome for protection, Rome need fear no power in the Hellenistic world. Hence the irresponsible and ruthless men who were coming to the fore at Rome in the middle of the second century B.C. saw no expedient reason — the only argument to which they might have given heed — for not administering the roughest treatment to Greeks who aroused their displeasure.

In the same fashion Acarnania, where the neutral party had committed the offense of arguing that Roman garrisons should not be introduced into a loyal and friendly country, was stripped of the island of Leucas, where the capital of the league was located. Thus Rome, controlling all the strategic island stepping-stones to the east as well as the principal land route, hoped to deter the Greeks from further demonstrations against her authority. In Epirus and Acarnania, as in Achaea and elsewhere in Greece, all individuals hostile to Rome, or suspected of being potentially hostile to Rome, were exiled to Italy — with the eager connivance of the pro-Roman parties, who thus saw their domestic ascendancy secured. With the aid of these parties, senatorial investigations, letters, and embassies, Rome henceforth controlled Epirus and Acarnania without interruption as far as we know, although Greece did not formally become a province until the reign of Augustus.

It is evident that the establishment of Roman hegemony in Epirus and Acarnania was a comparatively gradual process. From the Roman point of view this had been accomplished by 196, for Greece was only *libera,* not "free" in Roman eyes after that time. But since this policy rested on the guardianship of Greek *libertas* established in 196, it must have been conceived before that time; indeed, before the beginning of the Second Macedonian War, for the doctrine was ready when the war broke out. On the other hand, the real meaning of such terms as *libertas* and *amicitia* only gradually became clear to the Greeks. By 167 this meaning must have been clear to most of them, certainly to the Epirotes and Acarnanians; and such powers as these latter had no recourse but to accept it.

APPENDIX

THE ALLEGED ACARNANIAN APPEAL TO ROME

JUSTIN[1] SAYS that, presumably between 240 and 230 B.C., the Acarnanians asked Roman assistance against Aetolian aggression. According to Justin the Romans responded by sending an embassy to Aetolia, but without success. Indeed the Aetolians, not content with a response phrased with their usual insolence, shortly thereafter invaded and ravaged the Epirote and Acarnanian frontier districts. Justin gives at some length the text of a speech which purports to be the reply made by the Aetolians to the Romans on this occasion. A generation ago Maurice Holleaux[2] analyzed this passage of Justin exhaustively and concluded that there was no truth to the account whatever; that the entire passage was a tissue of falsehoods.

Holleaux's arguments still seem convincing; never, to my knowledge, has anyone attempted a point-by-point refutation of them. For example, the passage has against it the testimony of Polybius, both explicit and implied. Aside from Polybius' famous statement[3] that Rome's first diplomatic relations with the Greeks began in connection with the First Illyrian War, Holleaux[4] points out that the Acarnanian Lyciscus during the First Macedonian War (winter 211/10 B.C.) attempted to discredit the Aetolians on the ground that they had invited the Romans into Greece.[5] Lyciscus could not have used such an argument, or (granting the supposition that Polybius composed the speech himself) Polybius would not have put such an argument in Lyciscus' mouth, if the Acarnanians had previously invited the Romans into Greece. Besides, Holleaux shows that the whole passage in Justin and its context are bristling with difficulties and inconsistencies.[6]

Matthias Gelzer[7] agrees with Holleaux that Polybius did not have any knowledge of the Acarnanian appeal and the subsequent Roman embassy, but maintains that the episode is historical. Polybius, says Gelzer, was led to make his statement about Rome's first diplomatic and military contacts with the Greek homeland by his source, Fabius Pictor, who suppressed the whole incident as discreditable to Rome. But Gelzer makes no attempt to explain the difficulties Holleaux pointed out in detail; and it is very unsafe today to try to make out what a historian represented only by fragments omitted. Walther Kolbe[8] rejects Holleaux's view, but does not argue the question.[9]

According to Justin[10] the Acarnanians based their request to the Romans on the ground that they alone of the Greeks had not participated in the Greek war against the Trojan ancestors of the Romans; the Romans "qui denuntiarent Aetolis, praesidia ab urbibus Acarnaniae deducerent paterenturque liberos esse, qui soli quondam adversus Troianos, auctores originis suae, auxilia Graecis non miserint." A similar passage is to be found in Strabo:[11] Alone of the Greeks the Acarnanians did not participate in the Trojan War. "By following this account, it is likely (ὡς εἰκός) the Acarnanians tricked the Romans and obtained from them their autonomy (αὐτονομίαν), declaring that they alone had not participated in the expedition against the ancestors of the Romans." A slightly different story is recounted by Dionysius of Halicarnassus:[12] According to him, when Aeneas crossed the Ionian Sea from Greece to Italy, his pilots included Patron the Thyrian (Πάτρωνι τῷ Θουρίῳ).[13] In memory of this favor the Romans later (ἀνὰ χρόνον) gave the Acarnanians Leucas, Anactorium, and Oeniadae, "and to enjoy the produce (or revenues?) of the Echinades Islands jointly with the Aetolians." Polybius[14] says that the Aetolians were compelled to surrender Oeniadae to the Acarnanians as part of the settlement after the Aetolian (Syrian) War.

Generally speaking then, Justin, Strabo, and Dionysius agree that the Acarnanians received benefits from the Romans because of matters relating to the Trojan War. Justin and Strabo make this excuse nonparticipation in that conflict; Dionysius, services rendered Aeneas. All three apparently disagree as to what the benefits were. Dionysius says it was a grant of territory; Justin that it was diplomatic aid against the Aetolians; Strabo that it was the recognition of Acarnanian autonomy. Dionysius (partly) and Justin agree in making this favor granted by the Romans an action taken with reference to the Aetolians.

Holleaux[15] refers the origin of the tradition contained in the Justin passage to the Syrian-Aetolian War of 192-89 B.C. On the other hand he connects the granting of autonomy to Acarnania (the Strabo passage) with the settlement after the Second Macedonian War (196).[16] The cessions to Acarnania mentioned by Dionysius he puts partly in 197/6 (Leucas) and partly in 189

(Oeniadae).[17] This is probably correct. The statement in Dionysius is quite vague, chronologically, but leaves the impression that Leucas — and Anactorium! — were acquired by the Acarnanians at one time, and Oeniadae (and the share in the Echinades) later. But the statement about Leucas need mean no more than what is implied in Livy: that after Leucas surrendered upon the news of Cynoscephalae it was handed back to the Acarnanians.[18]

Holleaux, then, connected the Justin passage with the Aetolian (Syrian) War of 192-89 B.C., but dated the Strabo passage to 196. Yet the Strabo passage is decidedly similar in one respect to the Justin passage. Justin says that the Acarnanians procured a Roman request made to the Aetolians that the latter "paterentur ... liberos esse [Acarnanas]," the concrete sign of which would be that the Aetolians "praesidia ab urbibus Acarnaniae deducerent." That is to say, according to Justin, the Romans tried to procure Acarnanian independence from Aetolia, Aetolia being the power which was threatening that independence. But Strabo says that the Romans conferred autonomy on the Acarnanians. What exactly does "autonomy" mean in the passage? The word can mean full independence, or only one aspect or part of independence. Holleaux[19] points out that Strabo by "autonomy" means full independence, citing another passage in Strabo[20] where the latter says that the Aetolians and the Acarnanians long resisted Macedonians, other Greeks, and Romans in behalf of independence (αὐτονομίας).[21] Hence Holleaux says that "autonomy" does not equal "liberty" (*liberos*) as used by Justin. But the Justin passage must mean "liberty" in the general sense, not in the sense that the four Macedonian republics were *liberae* after 167 — "liberated" from arbitrary rule, or from a king's sway.[22] In Justin the Acarnanians are to be independent, free in the absolute sense, as the clause about the withdrawal of the *praesidia* shows.[23]

Moreover, Justin's work is the epitome of the *History* of Pompeius Trogus, but the sources of the latter were predominantly Greek — in first place Timagenes of Alexandria.[24] *Liberos* may well eventually represent some such Greek word as "autonomous." It proves nothing in itself, but it may not be out of place to mention that Strabo knew and used some, at least, of the works of Timagenes.[25]

In 189 the Aetolians were made by the Romans to give up

Oeniadae to the Acarnanians (and, if Dionysius may be trusted, to "enjoy" the Echinades islands with the latter). This would very well fit the provision, "praesidia ab urbibus Acarnaniae deducerent." It must be remembered that we are dealing with a highly distorted tradition. The fact of the cession of Oeniadae[26] could be distorted into a general statement regarding all Acarnanian cities held by the Aetolians at least as easily as the displacement of the "event" more than a generation backward in time.[27]

Conceivably the Justin-Strabo passages might refer to 197 and the period immediately following, when the Aetolians tried in vain to procure the cession to them of Leucas;[28] but as Holleaux has shown, the general tenor of the Justin passage fits better in the context of Aetolian open defiance of Rome at the time of the Syrian War. It might also be argued that in 197/6 the Acarnanians were in no particular position to ask Rome for favors after their stubborn adherence to Philip and their obstinate resistance on Leucas. For Rome to grant an unsolicited favor for her own reasons is another matter. Appeal to Rome on grounds of nonparticipation in the Trojan War fits better after 196 than in that year or before. In that year the people of Lampsacus appealed to Rome for aid on the ground that they were kinsmen of the Romans through the Trojans.[29] It would be more logical that appeal to the Romans on the ground of nonparticipation in the Trojan War should follow a favorably received appeal made on the grounds of kinship through Troy than that the reverse sequence should be correct. And the action taken by the Romans with regard to Acarnania after the Second Macedonian War falls at the latest in early 196.[30] Moreover, the Justin passage adds that the Aetolians after the Roman embassy ravaged the territories of Epirus as well as Acarnania.[31] In 197/6 the Aetolians had no reason for hostility to the Epirotes, but in 189 the Epirotes were at war with Aetolia.[32] After the resistance most of the Acarnanians had offered Antiochus in 190 they were in a better position to ask favors, and better acquainted with at least the externals of Roman policy in Greece. Most importantly, however, the Justin passage implies that the Aetolians are at the time of the request for aid in possession of the Acarnanian cities involved; "praesidia deducerentur." In 197 and afterward they did not hold Leucas but merely wished to acquire it.

If the preceding arguments be admitted, it is easy to theorize about the origin of the tradition. Acarnania received some gain (Oeniadae) at the Roman-Aetolian peace of 189. The Acarnanians had long wanted this city and the others that the Aetolians had obtained in the third century. It is probably safe to assume that they were not backward in pressing their claims before the Roman authorities, probably long before the end of the war. One of their arguments was their conduct during and after the Trojan War. For this appeal to the epic tradition they had at least the precedent of Lampsacus after the Second Macedonian War. What would be more natural than to suppose that various stories were bruited about as to what the Acarnanians were asking and what arguments they were using? This would account for the variations in detail contained in our three sources.

In turn we are confronted by the question of who originated the tradition, especially in the detailed and substantial form in which it appears in Justin with a date of about 240-230 B.C. Holleaux[33] declares that "the Roman character of the [Justin] tradition does not appear contestable." He sees in it an attempt to show the Romans as always mindful of benefits conferred upon their ancestors and to demonstrate that the Romans were always the refuge of the oppressed. Accordingly Holleaux believes that this legend was invented for the same purpose as the tale about a letter to King Seleucus which promised the Syrian monarch Roman friendship and alliance on condition he keep the people of Ilium free of all burdens.[34] But it seems very unlikely that any Roman annalist should have invented any episode so humiliating to the Romans as this case is made out to be. The Romans are made not only to fail of their object, but to receive a stinging and insulting rebuke; in addition their interference provokes an unpunished attack upon the people they have tried to befriend. As observed above, this episode can probably be traced behind Trogus-Justin to a Greek source, perhaps Timagenes. In this connection it may be noted that Timagenes, who lived in the latter part of the first century B.C., had quite a reputation for saucy hostility to the Romans.[35] Timagenes must have delighted in the speech put in the mouths of the Aetolians, if it did appear in his works. But Holleaux[36] himself has remarked how well this speech fits the insolence of the Aetolians so often employed at Roman expense in 192-189. I suggest, therefore, that the origin of the story is not only Greek, but possibly Aetolian — a specimen of the anti-Roman propaganda put about by the Aetolians.[37] One might well suppose that the Aetolians, learning that the Acarnanians were dickering with the Romans for the return of their lost cities, invented in substance the tale which we have in Justin, which shows their *intemperantia linguae* as Holleaux points out, and which shows that the Romans were impotent to fulfil any Acarnanian hopes of recovery of territory or even of protection. The garbled references to Roman history found in the speech fit well with the supposition that this is propaganda from a source not too well acquainted with Roman history.

Finally, there is nothing in any of these passages to lead one to assume any formal treaty between the Romans and the Acarnanians, who remained after 189, as before, simply "associates" (*socii*) of the Romans. The independence of Acarnania from Aetolian aggression was assured by the outcome of the Aetolian War and by the cession of Oeniadae (and possibly of some rights in the Echinades). Presumably now, however, the Acarnanians would be bound by the tie of gratitude to the Romans which the cession of Oeniadae and the end of the Aetolian menace created.

If the foregoing arguments be accepted, Holleaux is right in believing that the passage in Justin is to be related to the Syrian (Aetolian) War, but wrong in holding that the Strabo passage refers to a different period. Probably the passages in Dionysius, Justin, and Strabo are all variants of one tradition, and that tradition is hostile to Rome and a product of Greek, possibly Aetolian, propagandists. Holleaux had believed that the tradition (in Justin) had a Roman origin. The argument concerning the Trojan War, however, may well have actually been used by the Acarnanians *ca.* 190-189 B.C.

NOTES

Chapter I

1. See, for example, the discussion in F. W. Walbank, *Philip V of Macedon* (Cambridge [England], 1940), p. 149, n. 1 (continued on p. 150). For the topography of the Aous route see the description in J. Kromayer, *Antike Schlachtfelder in Griechenland. Bausteine zu einer antiken Kriegsgeschichte* (Berlin, 1907), II, 36-38. For the topography of Epirus in general see also map 2 at the end of the volume.
2. See the concise and suggestive remarks of A. W. Gomme, *A Historical Commentary on Thucydides,* I (Oxford, 1945), 19-29, anent the problems of ancient naval logistics.
3. Such a possibility was first suggested, I believe, by J. A. O. Larsen, "Roman Greece," *An Economic Survey of Ancient Rome,* ed. by Tenney Frank, IV (Baltimore, 1938), 259-498, at 275-76.
4. Cf. Eugen Oberhummer, *Akarnanien, Ambrakia, Amphilochien, Leukas im Altertum* (Munich, 1887), p. 175.
5. Cited by Strabo vii. 323 (No. 115 F 382, Jacoby, IIB). Cf. Martin P. Nilsson, "Studien zur Geschichte des alten Epeiros," *Lunds Universitets Årsskrift,* N.F., Afd. 1. VI, No. 4 (1909), 47, 49.
6. Cf. Carl Klotzsch, *Epirotische Geschichte bis zum Jahre 280 v. Chr.* (Berlin, 1911), p. 10, n. 1; G.N. Cross, *Epirus, A Study in Greek Constitutional Development* (Cambridge [England], 1932), p. 5, n. 1. On the importance of the Epirote tribes see Nilsson, *Årsskrift,* VI, No. 4, 47-48, cf. 67-68. The ethnic origin of the Epirotes is obscure. Nilsson (*ibid.*, 1-16) thought them non-Greek, but Vincenzo Constanzi ("La presunta egemonia dei Caoni nell' Epiro," *Atti della R. Accademia delle Scienze di Torino,* XLVII [1911-12], 969-77, at 974-77) and K. J. Beloch (*Griechische Geschichte* [4 vols., 2nd ed.; Berlin, 1912-27], I, Part 2, 33) vigorously reject this theory and maintain a largely Hellenic origin for the Epirotes. Cross, p. 2, n. 1, suggests that the Chaonians were not Greek, but that the Thesprotians and Molossians were mainly Hellenic. If so, ethnic differences may have helped inaugurate the tradition of particularism and regionalism among the Epirotes. On the other hand, perhaps the main reason for this particularism was geography. The mountains divide Epirus for the most part into fairly isolated valleys; cf. Nilsson, *Årsskrift,* VI, No. 4, 68.
7. Plutarch *Pyrrhus* 26. In general see Georg Busolt, *Griechische Staatskunde,* Part II (3rd ed., Munich, 1926), edited by Heinrich Swoboda, p. 1475 and nn.
8. So Cross, p. 99, n. 1.
9. Cf. M. I. Rostovtzeff, *The Social and Economic History of the Hellenistic World* (3 vols.; Oxford, 1941), II, 1162; 1163-64; III, 1609, n. 99. Nearly all Greek states raised grain, at least to some extent, and there is some evidence that Epirus was capable at times of producing a surplus (see below, p. 80).
10. Plutarch *Pyrrhus* 6. Unger's suggestion that the text of Plutarch be emended here to read "Atintania," or "Athamania," instead of "Acarnania," has met with little favor. Cf. W. W. Tarn, *Antigonos Gonatas*

(Oxford, 1913), p. 58, n. 53; Beloch, IV, Part 2, 383. Detailed discussion of the problem of determining the precise nature of Pyrrhus' control over Acarnania is to be found in Oberhummer (pp. 142-44), who thinks the passage should be emended to "Athamania," but also believes that Acarnania was part of Pyrrhus' dominions in some sense. See also Klotzsch, pp. 148 and n. 2 (acquisition dated to 294), 165, 171-75; Cross, pp. 130-31, 131, n. 3. Klotzsch, pp. 173-75, would seem to suppose that Pyrrhus was some sort of *hegemon* of the Acarnanian *koinon*.

11. Diodorus Siculus xix. 67. 3-5, 88. 2. Exactly what degree of importance should be attached to Cassander's acts in Acarnania at this time (314 B.C.) is a matter of some dispute. Cf. Oberhummer, pp. 214-15; E. Kirsten, *s.v.* "Oiniadai" (1), *RE*, XVII (1937), cols. 2204-28, at 2212; Rostovtzeff, I, 90. On the process of the Hellenization of the Adriatic Greek lands and the extension of Greek influence in that region in early times, see R. L. Beaumont, "Greek Influence in the Adriatic Sea Before the Fourth Century B.C.," *JHS*, LXVI (1936), 159-204.

12. Rostovtzeff, II, 1190.

13. On the Illyrians see Pompeius Trogus *Prologues* 25. Beloch, IV, Part 1, 595, suggests this connection between events in Illyria and Acarnania. There is no direct statement in the sources about the Acarnanians' severing their relationship with Epirus. We know only that shortly after this time they were independent (*IG*, IX², 1, 3A and B, later than the edition in *SIG³*, 421). On Epirus under Alexander and his successors see Cross, pp. 88 ff.

14. Cf. Robert Flacelière, *Les Aitoliens à Delphes, contributions à l'histoire de la Grèce centrale au III⁰ siècle av. J.-C.* (Paris, 1937), p. 192.

15. *IG*, IX², 1, 3A = *SIG³*, 421A, ll. 5 ff.

16. *Ibid.*, ll. 11-13.

17. *Ibid.*, ll. 27 ff.

18. Polybius ii. 45. 1, ix. 34. 7; Justin xxviii. 1. 1; Pausanias x. 16. 6; *IG*, IX², 1, 180; probably Frontinus *Strategemata* iii. 4. 5. On the boundaries see Oberhummer, pp. 145-46; Benedictus Niese, *Geschichte der griechischen und makedonischen Staaten seit der Schlacht bei Chaeronea* (3 vols.; Gotha, 1893-1903), II, 237. Possibly an obscure reference in Polybius relates to this partition (ix. 38. 9). If so, perhaps Antigonus Gonatas agreed not to interfere in the partition.

19. Günther Klaffenbach, "Die Zeit des ätolisch-arkarnanischen Bündnisvertrages," *Klio*, XXIV (1931), 223-34; accepted at least in part by Cross, pp. 131-32, and Max Cary, *A History of the Greek World From 323 to 146 B.C.* (New York, 1939), pp. 145-46 and 146, n. 2. Klaffenbach's entire line of argument has been rejected, however, by Flacelière, p. 192 and n. 4.

20. Niese, II, 237 and n. 7, believes that the Acarnanians under Alexander retained their local "Stammverfassung" (as, Niese thinks, they had under Pyrrhus). I know of no evidence for this; unless we follow the older view (with Flacelière) that Acarnania was partitioned before the Chremonidean War, and unless we believe that when Justin (xxvi. 3. 1) says that Alexander was restored to the throne of Epirus "auxilio sociorum," the Acarnanians, to whom he had fled, are meant. Then *socii* would describe Acarnania under Epirote rule. A consideration that militates

against Niese's view is that there is reason for believing that in 231 B.C. the Acarnanian *koinon* was not in existence (see below, n. 41).

21. Justin xxvi. 2. 9-11, 3.1. The statement that Antigonus lost his own kingdom for a time to Alexander is probably an exaggeration. Beloch, IV, Part 2, 504-6, argues that Alexander's attack on Macedonia did not occur during the Chremonidean War (*i.e.*, Justin is mistaken), but at about the time of the death of Magas of Cyrene, which he places *ca.* 250 B.C. Justin, after narrating this exploit of Alexander, goes on to say that "per idem tempus" Magas died. But Cary, pp. 393-94, shows that Magas must have died several years before 250. Furthermore, in addition to the arguments advanced by Cary, it is easier to believe that Justin is exaggerating in the vague phrase, "per idem tempus," than that he is mistaken when he states that Alexander's intervention in Macedonia occurred in connection with the Chremonidean War. Such a conjunction of events would be more likely to be gotten straight than a temporal coincidence involving unrelated events in distant Cyrenaica.

22. Giuseppe Corradi, "Gli ultimi Eacidi," *Atti della R. Accademia delle Scienze di Torino*, XLVII (1911-12), 192-215, at 197-200; Niese, II, 264; Walbank, *Philip V*, p. 295 (for the birth of Philip, son of Demetrius and Phthia, whose marriage probably soon followed the death of Alexander — Philip's birth is dated to 238); W. W. Tarn, "Phthia-Chryseis," *Athenian Studies Presented to W. S. Ferguson, Harvard Studies in Classical Philology*, Suppl. Vol. I (1940), 483-501, at 490-91 (Demetrius-Phthia marriage dated winter 239/8); Sterling Dow and C. F. Edson, Jr., "Chryseis," *Harvard Studies in Classical Philology*, XLVIII (1937), 127-80, at 158 (Demetrius-Phthia marriage dated in 239/8 or 238/7); Flacelière, 245; W. W. Tarn, "The Greek Leagues and Macedonia," *CAH*, VII (Cambridge [England], 1928), 732-68, at 733; Maurice Holleaux, "The Romans in Illyria," *ibid.*, 822-57, at 828.

23. Justin xxviii. 1. 1-3. For the supposed appeal of the Acarnanians to Rome about this time and an alleged embassy of the Romans to Aetolia in response (Justin xxviii. 1. 5-2. 14), see below, Appendix, pp. 92-97.

24. Fortunately it is not necessary for the present purpose to enter into the tangled question of the relationships of the last members of the royal family of Epirus to each other. The sources are: Polybius vii. 4. 5; Livy xxiv. 6. 8; Athenaeus xiii. 589-90; Helladius cited by Photius, *Bibliotheca*, p. 530a 27-29 (Bekker); Polyaenus viii. 52; Trogus *Prologues* 28; Justin xxviii. 3; Pausanias iv. 35. 3, 5; Ovid *Ibis* 303-8; George Syncellus, *Chronographia*, p. 578 (Bonn). Arguments have also been based on SIG^3, 453, but Piero Treves, "La tradizione politica degli Antigonidi e l'opera di Demetrio II," *Rendiconti della R. Accademia Nazionale dei Lincei*, Classe di scienze morali, storiche, e filologiche, 6th series, VIII (1932), 167-205, at 201, n. 2, rightly points out that it is completely inconclusive. There have been numereous attempts at reconciliation of these late and contradictory accounts; *e.g.*, Corradi, *Atti di Torino*, XLVII (1911-12), 192-215; Niese, II, 196; Oberhummer, pp. 149-51; Beloch, IV, Part 2, 150-51; Cross, pp. 124-27. In this maze of late and confused sources the irreducible implication of Polybius that Nereis, who married Gelo of Syracuse, was the daughter of Pyrrhus I must stand (*contra* Beloch and others). Cross, p. 125, points out that if Nereis was a daughter of the great Pyrrhus she must have been about forty when

she married for the first time, since she was a "virgo" when she married Gelo, as Justin (xxviii. 3. 4) expressly tells us. Further, Cross says that first marriages of Hellenistic princesses at that age were quite unusual. True, but if there was not something unusual about Nereis' being a *virgo* when she married, why should Justin, or Trogus, or their source, mention the fact? Justin does not regularly record that princesses of Epirus were *virgines* when they first married. Why specify this in the case of Nereis?

25. "Laudamia" in Justin is erroneous or, more probably, a corruption.
26. W. W. Tarn, "The Social Question in the Third Century," *The Hellenistic Age,* by J. B. Bury *et al.* (Cambridge [England], 1925), pp. 108-140; *idem, Hellenistic Civilization* (3rd ed. rev. by author and G. T. Griffith; London, 1952), pp. 121 ff.; Rostovtzeff, I, 209; II, 610; and *passim;* J. A. O. Larsen, *Economic Survey,* IV, 421-22.
27. Athenaeus xiii. 589-90; Helladius cited by Photius, *Bibliotheca,* p. 530a 27-29 (Bekker); Ovid *Ibis* 307-8.
28. Justin xxviii. 3. 5-8; Pausanias iv. 35. 3, 5; Polyaenus viii. 52. The sources give short and conflicting accounts of events; various reconstructions can be found in Oberhummer, p. 151; Niese, II, 266; Cross, p. 96. See also the references to secondary works above, n. 24.
29. xxviii. 3. 7.
30. iv. 35. 5.
31. The revolution is an accomplished fact by 230 when the Illyrians seized Phoenice, for in discussing the events connected with the capture of the city Polybius (ii. 5. 3 ff.) gives no hint of the continuance of open strife in Epirus. On the other hand the revolution comes after the alliance of Epirus and Macedonia and the marriage of Demetrius of Macedonia with Phthia-Chryseis about 239. The various vicissitudes of the royal family — the deaths of Olympias and her wards and the marriage of Nereis, which left Deidameia alone — probably occupied some years after 239. Hence about 234 or 233 seems approximately correct. See also F. W. Walbank, *Aratos of Sicyon* (Cambridge [England], 1933), p. 185. Oberhummer, p. 151, puts the revolution in 236. Such a date is of course possible, but sandwiches the various misadventures of the royal house between the alliance with Macedonia and the revolution into a perhaps excessively brief period. Beloch, IV, Part 1, 635, puts the revolution in *ca.* 231 B.C., but it must be remembered that he dates the First Illyrian War a year late, and thus postpones all events chronologically related to it by a year. On the difficulties of the chronology see also Treves, *Rendiconti Lincei,* 6th series, VIII (1932), 196.
32. *Praetores,* Livy xxix. 12. 11.
33. *SGDI,* 1338, 1339, 1349, 1350.
34. Busolt-Swoboda, II, 1477. It has been suggested that the three generals represent the three major Epirote tribes: Molossians, Thesprotians, Chaonians (cf. E. A. Freeman, *History of Federal Government in Greece and Italy,* ed. by J. B. Bury [2nd ed.; London, 1893], p. 118). Freeman *(ibid.)* thinks that Livy xxxii. 10. 2 may indicate a change from three generals to one. Such a change is by no means impossible, and one general would be more typical of Hellenistic federalism, but the passage in ques-

tion may mean only that one of the generals acted alone in this case, perhaps the eponymous member of the college.

35. For what our scanty sources tell us about the government of Epirus, see Busolt-Swoboda, II, 1475-77.
36. See J. A. O. Larsen, "Representation and Democracy in Hellenistic Federalism," *CP*, XL (1945), 65-97, at 88-91; cf. André Aymard, "L'organisation de la Macédoine en 167 et le régime représentatif dans le monde grec," *ibid.*, XLV (1950), 96-107, at 102 and n. 33.
37. Polybius ii. 5. 3 ff.
38. Polybius ii. 7. 11.
39. Polybius ii. 6. 11-7. 12. Cross, p. 96 and n. 3, suggests that these mercenaries may originally have been sent by Hiero of Syracuse to protect the monarchy. Polybius (ii. 7. 10), however, expressly says that they had been expelled from Italy by the Romans. Epirus offered them a perfect place to fish in recently troubled waters.
40. Justin xxviii. 4. 12-15, esp. 13; cf. Tarn, *CAH*, VII (1928), 759.
41. There is no direct evidence concerning Acarnanian revindication of independence. Acarnania is represented by Polybius (ii. 6. 9) as independent in 230 B.C. In 231 the Aetolians made their famous attack on Medion (*ibid.*, 2. 5 ff.), which is probably to be presumed independent at that juncture. Possibly, however, the Acarnanian League had not been re-formed at that time, for Polybius seems to represent the people of Medion as acting alone against the Aetolians. Following this reasoning, Oberhummer (pp. 157-58) puts the founding of the new league in 231/0. Most scholars, at any rate, connect the independence of Acarnania with the decline and fall of the monarchy in Epirus; *e.g.*, Beloch, IV, Part 2, 384; Oberhummer, p. 152; Maurice Holleaux, *Rome, la Grèce et les monarchies hellénistiques au III° siècle avant J.-C. (273-205)* (Paris, 1921), pp. 11-12.
42. Livy xxxiii. 17. 1.
43. For "The Thousand" see *IvM*, 31, 1. 27, and in general, on the government of Acarnania, Busolt-Swoboda, II, 1468-69.
44. W. Schwahn, *s.v.* "Συμπολιτεία (Geschichte)," *RE*, IVA (1932), cols. 1194-99, at 1198, believes that Acarnania became a true democracy and that the term "The Thousand" had "nur noch eine historische Bedeutung," but he cites no evidence and a trend toward true democracy in the Hellenistic age would be very surprising. Busolt's inference (Busolt-Swoboda, II, 1469) about hoplite suffrage is strengthened by the reference to 1,000 Acarnanian hoplites contained in the Aetolian-Acarnanian treaty, *IG*, IX², 1, 3A.
45. Ambracia was in Epirote hands up to the time of the murder of Deidameia (Polyaenus viii. 52).
46. Polybius iv. 61. 6.
47. Niese, II, 267, and n. 6, puts the loss of Ambracia about 230. Oberhummer, p. 152 and n. 2, dates it after 230, for he thinks that the Epirotes would not have appealed to the Aetolians as they did in that year, had the latter taken Ambracia shortly before. Beloch, IV, Part 2, 384, concurs. See also Cesare Salvetti, "Ricerche storiche intorno alla lega etolica," *Studi di storia antica*, II (1893), 95-137 at 107, 115. The opinion

of Oberhummer and Beloch is by no means impossible, but on the other hand it must be borne in mind that the need of the Epirotes was desperate. They might have swallowed their pride and appealed to Aetolia even if she had acquired Ambracia shortly before. Tarn, *CAH*, VII (1928), 748, connects the loss of Ambracia with the Illyrian raid on Epirus in 230, as does Flacelière, p. 252.

48. See the references cited in the preceding note. Flacelière, pp. 257-58 and 258, n. 1, points out that Amynander (usually identified with the Amynas of Polybius iv. 16. 9), king of Athamania, was probably the ally of the Aetolians in 220 (Polybius iv. 16. 9-10), and supposes that Athamania also became independent of Epirus about 230 (p. 296, n. 3) and an ally of Aetolia. So also Tarn, *CAH*, VII (1928), 748. Beloch, IV, Part 2, 378f., thought that Tymphaea and Parauaea (districts in the northeast of Epirus) were lost to Macedonia sometime between the death of Pyrrhus I and the Epirote revolution. His views have been refuted by J. V. A. Fine, "The Problem of Macedonian Holdings in Epirus and Thessaly in 221 B.C.," *TAPA*, LXIII (1932), 126-55, at 127-29. Fine shows that the two districts were in Epirote hands in 199-98 B.C.

49. So Tarn, *CAH*, VII (1928), 747; Treves, *Rendiconti Lincei*, 6th series, VIII (1932), 196, 204.

50. On the supposed alliance of Epirus with Aetolia shortly after the revolution see below, n. 58. Treves, *ibid.*, 167-205, and "Studi su Antigono Dosone," *Athenaeum*, 2nd series, XII (1934), 381-411; XIII (1935), 22-56, has built on these inferences a large pyramid of conjecture and assumption which aims at showing that Demetrius II of Macedonia was in process of building up a series of alliances not only against Aetolia but against Rome as well. According to Treves (*Rendiconti Lincei*, 6th series, VIII [1932], 201) the marriage of Nereis to Gelo of Syracuse was part of a plan to bring Syracuse into an anti-Roman combination (cf. *ibid.*, pp. 202-3). Walbank, *Philip V*, p. 12, n. 4, rightly labels this theory an extreme form of Holleaux's thesis that Macedonia was alarmed by the Roman "protectorate" in the Balkans (229 B.C. ff.). Treves has simply extended Macedonian anti-Roman feeling into the previous period, without justification, it seems to me.

51. From this point onward it will be convenient to understand by this term independent Acarnania, the part that Alexander II had added to his dominions and that later had become free about 230.

52. Polybius ii. 2. 6.

53. Presumably the people of Medion alone sent the appeal for aid, if we accept the reasoning of Oberhummer that Polybius' failure to mention the Acarnanian *koinon* means that the federal government had not been set up as yet; see above, n. 41.

54. Polybius ii. 2. 4-3. 8.

55. Or rather, presumably somewhere along the coast near by, since Phoenice stands inland from the sea.

56. Polybius ii. 7. 5-10.

57. Polybius ii. 4. 6-5. 8.

58. Polybius ii. 6. 1-2, cf. 6. 9. On the basis of Polybius ii. 6. 1, Beloch, IV, Part 1, 635, concluded that the Epirotes already had an alliance with

Aetolia and appealed to the latter on the ground of this treaty. But there is nothing in this passage to warrant such an assumption. If the passage shows that there was such a pre-existing treaty, it is also evidence for a pre-existing treaty with Achaea as well, and this is unlikely. If anything, the language of Polybius implies that there was no treaty; the Epirotes "asked as suppliants." One of the most famous episodes in ancient history is the appeal of the Corcyraeans for assistance to Athens shortly before the great Peloponnesian War. Had Thucydides not given us a detailed account of the proceedings, and simply told us that the Corcyraeans asked for and received aid, would we be justified in supposing a previous alliance between Corcyra and Athens on that ground? In 230 the need of the Epirotes was pressing: of their neighbors the Illyrians were their foes; Macedonia was the ally of Illyria, was ill-disposed to the Epirotes, and was unable to help anyway; the Acarnanians were probably well-disposed to the Illyrians after the affair at Medion. That left only Aetolia and Achaea to whom the Epirotes could appeal. Maurice Holleaux, "La politique romaine en Grèce et dans l'Orient hellénistique au IIIe siècle. Réponse à M. Th. Walek," *Revue de philologie, de littérature et d'histoire anciennes*, L (1926), 46-66, 194-218, at 51 and n. 2, saw this a quarter-century ago.

59. Polybius ii. 6. 1-8.
60. Polybius ii. 5. 1, 8. 1; cf. 4. 6.
61. Polybius ii. 6. 7-8.
62. Polybius makes no mention of the cession of Atintania, but he strongly implies (ii. 5. 6; cf. 5. 8) that in 230 it was in Epirote hands. Yet during the next year, when the Romans were making war on the Illyrians, Atintania went over to the Romans (Polybius ii. 11. 11). Appian *Illyrica* ii. 7 says that Agron (this must be wrong; understand Teuta) acquired part of Epirus; this could well mean Atintania. So Beloch, IV, Part 2, 380-81, reasoned; cf. Cary, p. 400; Maurice Holleaux, "The Romans in Illyria," *CAH,* VII (1928), 822-57, at 831; idem, *Rome,* p. 110, n. 1. The objections of Tarn, *Antigonos Gonatas,* p. 312, n. 3, are not convincing.
63. Polybius ii. 6. 9-10.
64. On a voyage to Egypt in the middle of the third century, the Achaean statesman Aratus traveled part of the way on a "Roman" ship (Plutarch *Aratus* 12). Probably it would be better to understand "Italian" for "Roman." On the Italians in the East in the third century see Jean Hatzfeld, *Les trafiquants italiens dans l'Orient hellénique* (Paris, 1919), p. 18.
65. Polybius ii. 8. 1. Tenney Frank, *Roman Imperialism* (New York, 1925), p. 111, suggests that the Roman colony of Aesis, founded shortly after the beginning of the First Punic War, was intended to discourage the pirates.
66. On the importance of Corcyra as a center for marine communications between east and west, see Thucydides i. 36. 2, 37. 3; T. J. Dunbabin, *The Western Greeks* (Oxford, 1948), pp. 194-95.
67. For Corcyra perhaps the most easily accessible map is in Gomme, I, facing p. 196, but unfortunately it does not include the whole island.
68. Polybius ii. 8. 2.
69. For the chronology see Maurice Holleaux, "Études d'histoire hellénistique. La date de la première guerre romaine d'Illyrie," *REG,* XLIII (1930),

243-61; summarized by Holleaux, *CAH,* VII (1928), 834, n. 1, in answer to Beloch, IV, Part 1, 664 ff., who puts all these events one year later.

70. Polybius ii. 8. 6-13. In implying that Rome was reluctantly forced into war by force of circumstances I have followed Holleaux, *CAH,* VII (1928), 824-38, esp. 832; *idem, Rome,* pp. 98-109. The most thoroughgoing criticisms of Holleaux's conclusions have been put forward by Piero Treves, especially in *Athenaeum,* XII (1934), 388-91. See also Treves in *Rendiconti Lincei,* 6th series, VIII (1932), 167-205, and Treves' reviews of F. W. Walbank's *Aratos of Sicyon* (*Athenaeum,* 2nd series, XII [1934], 324-29) and of Walbank's *Philip V* (*JHS,* LXIII [1943], 117-20). Holleaux has also been criticized by Tadeusz Walek-Czernecki, "La politique romaine en Grèce et dans l'Orient hellénistique au IIIe siècle," *Revue de philologie, de littérature et d'histoire anciennes,* XLIX (1925), 28-54. Holleaux himself ably refuted Walek's views, *ibid.,* L (1926), 46-66, 194-218. Walek seems also to have expounded his views in a book entitled *Dzieje upadku monarchji macedonskiej* [*History of the Fall of the Macedonian Monarchy,* with a French summary] (Cracow, 1924), but this book has not been available to me. Walek (especially) and Treves depend too much on the *argumentum ex silentio* and on arbitrary rejection of inconvenient evidence. Holleaux, in my opinion, offers the best interpretation of what evidence we have, and beyond that it is impossible to go. Walek himself has offered the best criticism of his own thesis. Speaking of the date of Aetolian-Roman treaty of 212 or 211 B.C., he remarks, "Il est d'abord à remarquer que l'opinion ayant en sa faveur la tradition antique est *a priori* préférable et qu'il faudrait des raisons péremptoires pour accepter la thèse opposée." (Walek, "La chronologie de la première guerre de Macédoine," *Revue de philologie, de littérature et d'histoire anciennes,* LIV [1928], 5-24 at 9.) For an answer to Treves, see André Aymard, "Antigonus Doson," *REA,* XXXVIII (1936), 265-67, esp. 267, n. 1.

On the supposed appeal of the island of Issa to the Romans as a cause of the First Illyrian War, see the objections of Holleaux, *Rome,* p. 23, n. 6. Gaetano de Sanctis, *Storia dei Romani* (Turin, 1907 ff.), III, Part 1, 295 and n. 86 accepts the tale, however, as does Matthias Gelzer, "Römische Politik bei Fabius Pictor," *Hermes,* LXVIII (1933), 129-66, at 143-44.

The Romans went first to Corcyra; therefore it has been concluded that their object could not have been merely the punishment of Teuta; according to Gelzer the move to Corcyra demonstrates that the Romans had a good knowledge of the situation. The Romans had then been investigating the trans-Adriatic situation thoroughly, with the help of the people of Issa. It is quite true that the descent on Corcyra shows the Romans had a good grasp of the situation; the Illyrians had but shortly before accepted the surrender of the island. But Roman awareness of the situation need only indicate that the Roman intelligence system was functioning well; but a bit slowly, since the quarry had departed when the Romans arrived. The source of Roman information might well be the Italiote Greek traders who regularly sailed these waters and were very interested in stopping Illyrian piracy. In any event Corcyra, center of lower Adriatic marine communications, was a logical place for the Romans to make for first.

71. Polybius ii. 9-10.
72. Polybius ii. 10. 1.
73. Polybius ii. 11.
74. Polybius ii. 11.
75. Appian *Illyrica* 7.
76. Holleaux, *Rome*, p. 106, n. 2; cf. Livy xxiv. 40, xxvi. 25. 2; Zonaras ix. 4. 4.
77. Cf. Larsen, *Economic Survey*, IV, 262-63.
78. ii. 12. 3.
79. *Illyrica* 7. On Appian's trustworthiness here, see Larsen, *Economic Survey*, IV, 262.
80. *Phoros:* usually "tribute," but here "indemnity"; cf. Beloch, IV, Part 1, 666; and Larsen, *Economic Survey*, IV, 262.
81. Ὑπηκόους.
82. The Romans are called κύριοι of these places in vii. 9. 13; these places are τὰς ὑπὸ 'Ρωμαίους ταττομένας in iii. 16. 3.
83. Polybius ii. 11; for the meaning of *deditio* cf. xx. 9. 12, xxxvi. 4. 1-3.
84. Alfred Heuss, *Die völkerrechtlichen Grundlagen der römischen Aussenpolitik in republikanischer Zeit, Klio*, Beiheft XXXI (Leipzig, 1933), p. 61; Eugen Täubler, *Imperium Romanum, Studien zur Entwickelungsgeschichte des römischen Reichs*, I (Leipzig, 1913), p. 15. Deditio = deditio in fidem (εἰς πίστιν), Täubler, pp. 16-17; for the Greek translations of the Latin terms, *ibid.*, p. 26 and n. 3.
85. Heuss, pp. 62-63, 69-70.
86. Heuss, pp. 78-83.
87. See Heuss, pp. 94 ff., for the legal aspect; with the remarks of J. A. O. Larsen, "Was Greece Free Between 196 and 146 B.C.?" *CP*, XXX (1935), 193-214, at 196-97 and nn., for the practical considerations.
88. Appian *Illyrica* 8; Strabo vii. fr. 8. Exactly when these various states passed from *deditio* to *libertas* is uncertain. Probably it was after only a very short time, for in this period *dediticii* very seldom remained long in that condition (Heuss, pp. 71-72). Polybius (ii. 11. 11) says that the Romans admitted the Atintanians and Parthinians to "friendship" in 229, but he may not be speaking with strict technical accuracy.
89. *CAH*, VII, 836-37; cf. *Rome*, pp. 105-6.
90. Notoriously the Aetolians didn't understand such matters a generation later; cf. Larsen, *CP*, XXX (1935), 198 and n. 24.
91. Larsen, *ibid.*, p. 199; cf. G. Zippel, *Die römische Herrschaft in Illyrien bis auf Augustus* (Leipzig, 1877), p. 91.
92. I am following Polybius (ii. 12. 2); it is quite possible, however, that it was Fulvius who stayed in Greece; see De Sanctis, *Storia*, III, Part 1, 297, n. 89.
93. We have no evidence for Roman favor extended to the "upper" classes in the "protectorate," but Rome had long favored the men of substance in Italy, as she was to do later in Greece itself. It is reasonable to assume that her policy was not different in the "protectorate."
94. Holleaux, *CAH*, VII, 838, argued that a reason for the establishment of

the "protectorate" was "to isolate the kingdom of Illyria from its new Greek allies, the Epirotes and Acarnanians."
95. Polybius ii. 12. 4, 8.

Chapter II

1. This view is that of Maurice Holleaux, *CAH,* VII, 837-40; *idem, Rome,* pp. 104-12; of Eduard Meyer, "Hannibal und Scipio," *Meister der Politik. Eine weltgeschichtliche Reihe von Bildnissen,* ed. by Erich Marcks and K. A. von Müller, I (2nd ed.; Stuttgart, 1923), 99-146, at 107-8; *idem,* "Die römische Politik vom ersten bis zum Ausbruch des zweiten punischen Krieges," *Kleine Schriften,* II (Halle, 1924), 375-401, at 394; of K. J. Beloch, IV, Part 1, 667; and of Gaetano de Sanctis, *Storia dei Romani,* III, Part 2, 398. This view has also been followed by W. W. Tarn, *CAH,* VII, 765; and by M. I. Rostovtzeff, I, 48; but it has been challenged recently by Max Cary, p. 406; and by F. W. Walbank, *Philip V,* pp. 12 and n. 4; 64-5 and the earlier portion of the book, *passim;* cf. *idem, Aratos of Sicyon,* p. 152. Cary and Walbank have in effect returned to the view of Tenney Frank (cf. *Roman Imperialism,* p. 160, n. 9) that Macedonia was not particularly concerned by the Roman "protectorate" along the Adriatic.
2. See his works cited in the preceding note.
3. Cf. Thucydides ii. 80. 7.
4. Cary, p. 406, minimizes these instances of interference in western politics. True, the rulers of Macedonia did not continually try to make their influence felt in the west; they had other commitments which were more pressing: in Greece, in the Aegean, in the north, and in Macedonia itself. Except for Pyrrhus' "Empire" (which had certainly harassed Gonatas) there had never been any real danger to Macedonia in the west, because there had been no great power there. Precisely after 229, I believe, the west became a primary issue at Pella.
5. See above, p. 5.
6. Holleaux, *Rome,* p. 102, n. 3, accepted by Walek-Czernecki, *Revue de philologie, de littérature, et d'histoire anciennes,* XLIX (1925), 41-42.
7. Holleaux, *Rome,* p. 120, suggests that this lack of diplomatic courtesy indicates that Postumius (or the senate) was convinced that no accommodation with Macedonia was possible. Possibly also the Romans wished to avoid Macedonian recriminations and an "international incident."
8. *Storia,* III, Part 1, 327.
9. Cf. Holleaux, *Rome,* p. 120.
10. Further than this it probably would not be safe to go, but it is tempting to speculate that Antigonus Doson may have been the more favorably inclined to a renewal of friendly relations with the Epirotes because he wished to strengthen his position in the west as much as possible. If this be so, the alliance of Doson with Epirus is particular proof of his western interests.
11. Polybius iv. 9. 4, 15. 1.

12. Polybius xi. 5. 4; and see Walbank, *Philip V,* p. 16, n. 3.
13. Polybius iv. 9. 4, cf. ii. 54. 4; Plutarch *Aratus* 42-43.
14. Polybius ii. 65. 4.
15. It may be noted in passing that new members could not be received into the league without the consent of the king and the rest of the allies (Polybius iv. 9. 3).
16. Livy xxxii. 22. 3.
17. W. S. Ferguson, *Greek Imperialism* (Boston, 1913), p. 244, accepted by Larsen (see below, n. 19).
18. Plutarch *Aratus* 45. It is unfortunate that we probably do not know exactly how this prohibition was worded; whether "with any other king," or "with any other state," or "with any other state not in Greece proper." Probably, however, Plutarch is speaking literally, and the provision was meant to exclude tampering with the allies by the Antigonids' rivals in the Hellenistic world, notably of course the Ptolemies.
19. Polybius iv. 24. 4. For the constitution of the league see the discussions by J. A. O. Larsen, "Representative Government in the Panhellenic Leagues," *CP,* XX (1925), 313-29; XXI (1926), 52-71; at XXI, 66-69; Busolt-Swoboda, II, 1395. There is also a brief statement in Walbank, *Philip V,* pp. 15-18; other discussions are cited *ibid.,* p. 15, n. 6.
20. See above, p. 7, and Walbank, *Philip V,* p. 17.
21. It was not finally dissolved until the Second Macedonian War, and then under Roman compulsion; see below, pp. 44, 52.
22. Treves, *Athenaeum,* 2nd series, XIII (1935), 37, maintains that the primary motive of the league was anti-Roman. On Treves' interpretation of virtually all Doson's major activities as marks of an anti-Roman policy, see the criticisms of André Aymard, "Antigonus Doson," *REA,* XXXVIII (1936), 265-67.
23. Even if one could trust the exact language of Plutarch, it would be unsafe to try to build any hypothesis relating to Rome on this clause.
24. Polybius ii. 11. 17; Appian *Illyrica* 8.
25. Polybius ii. 66. 5, cf. iii. 16. 3.
26. Polybius iii. 16. 2; Appian *Illyrica* 8. Cf. Holleaux, *Rome,* p. 131, n. 5; Niese, II, 326, 417. Another indication that Doson was interesting himself in the Adriatic coastlands.
27. Polybius iii. 16. 3.
28. *Illyrica* 8.
29. Th. Büttner-Wobst, *s.v.* "Demetrius" (44a), *RE,* Supp. I (1903), cols. 342-45, at 344, doubts the authenticity of Appian's statement.
30. Polybius iv. 16. 6-8.
31. Polybius iii. 16. 7, iii. 18-19, iv. 66. 4. There are also discussions of little worth in the late Roman sources: Appian *Illyrica* 8; Zonaras viii. 20. 11-13; *De viris illustribus* 50; Frontinus *Strategemata* iv. 1. 45 (?). On these sources see Holleaux, *Rome,* p. 138, n. 2; Niese, II, 436, n. 4; 437, n. 2; Beloch, IV, Part 1, 732, n. 3.
32. Polybius iii. 18. 1.
33. iii. 16. 2.

34. Holleaux, *Rome*, p. 141.
35. iv. 16. 1.
36. Holleaux, *Rome*, p. 141 and n. 4.
37. By J. V. A. Fine, "Macedon, Illyria, and Rome," *JRS*, XXVI (1936), 24-39, at 31-33 and 38-39. Fine's conclusions have been accepted by Walbank, *Philip V*, p. 28, n. 7.
38. Polybius iv. 87. 6-8.
39. Polybius iii. 16. 4. Cf. Holleaux, *CAH*, VII, 848. For the view that the Second Illyrian War was an adventure of Roman imperialism, see Walek, *Revue de philologie, de littérature et d'histoire anciennes*, XLIX (1925), 42 ff.; ably answered by Holleaux, *ibid.*, L (1926), 46-66, 194-218.
40. Cf. Holleaux, *Rome*, pp. 137-38.
41. Treves, *Athenaeum*, 2nd series, XIII (1935), 44-46 much exaggerates, I think, the importance of Doson's alliance with Demetrius. I have tried to show, instead, that Doson was merely making certain general preparations for the indefinite future.
42. Cf. Polybius vii. 9. 13; Larsen, *Economic Survey*, IV, 262-63.
43. Why the Romans did not also deal firmly with Scerdilaidas, equally guilty with Demetrius of breaking the treaty with Rome, is a mystery. One can only suggest that perhaps Rome felt that the treatment of Demetrius would serve as a warning to Scerdilaidas as well; and that to punish Scerdilaidas would prolong the war unduly and thus increase the opportunity for Macedonia to interfere, while at the same time the attention of the Roman government was becoming increasingly engrossed in the affairs of Spain. See also De Sanctis, *Storia*, III, Part 1, 325.
44. Walbank, *Philip V*, pp. 295-99.
45. Polybius iv. 3. 2-4.
46. Polybius iv. 6. 2, cf. 5. 10.
47. Polybius iv. 15. 1-2.
48. Polybius iv. 15. 8-10; cf. Walbank, *Philip V*, p. 27.
49. Polybius iv. 16. 1-3 mentions only the Epirotes and Philip; but the answer of the rest of the allies must have been similar, cf. Walbank, *Philip V*, p. 28, n. 2.
50. See preceding note, and above, pp. 21-22.
51. Fine, *JRS*, XXVI (1936), 38-39.
52. Walbank, *Philip V*, p. 28.
53. Polybius iv. 16-21.
54. Polybius iv. 19. 1.
55. This accords with the view that Philip had inspired the previous negative answer of the allies to the Achaean request for league assistance, for obviously the allies still harbored resentment at these wrongs.
56. Polybius iv. 25.
57. See above, p. 8.
58. See above, p. 4.
59. Polybius iv. 30. 2.
60. Polybius iv. 30. 6-7. Polybius goes on (iv. 30. 8) immediately after

this passage to say that envoys were sent to King Ptolemy asking him to remain completely neutral. This latter passage has been taken to mean that the Epirotes sent the envoys (Niese, II, 424; Schwahn, *RE*, IVA, col. 1241), but this is very unlikely. Entirely apart from the fact that it apparently would violate the provision of the league covenant regarding negotiations with foreign kings, such an action would imply that the Epirotes had a much warmer interest in the war than they actually did have, since there is no reason to believe that Ptolemy was particularly concerned with Epirus at this time. A closer reading of the passage shows that the ambassadors were sent by the Hellenic League (cf. Polybius iv. 26, 30. 1, 31. 1). Walbank, *Philip V*, p. 36, n. 2, is as ambiguous as Polybius.

61. We hear of no Aetolian embassy to Acarnania. Had there been one, it would have been repulsed, and Polybius would not have failed to mention such a repulse in his eulogy of Acarnanian constancy and honor (Polybius iv. 30. 2-5). The inference is that the Aetolians thought there was a chance Epirus might be won over, but not Acarnania.

62. Walbank, *Philip V*, pp. 38 ff., minimizes this aspect of the war, inasmuch as he believes it was not until 217 that Philip suddenly resolved to attack Rome. I have previously discussed the reasons why I think this view should be rejected. If, as I believe, it was the policy of Doson and Philip eventually to do something about the "protectorate" when they had the opportunity, it is logical to assume that one of the reasons why Philip wished to win the lasting friendship of the Epirotes was that he was keeping the eventual contingency of an attack on the "protectorate" in mind. I do not wish to imply that at this time Philip had already determined to settle his accounts with the Romans. See Fine, *JRS*, XXVI (1936), 35, 38.

63. Polybius iv. 61. 1-63. 4.

64. Polybius iv. 63. 7, 10, 64. 4, 65. 5.

65. Polybius iv. 63. 7-8.

66. Polybius iv. 65. 5-11. The ruins of these fortifications at Oeniadae are still to be seen; see E. Kirsten, *RE*, XVII, cols. 2223 ff.; Benjamin Powell, 'Oeniadae. I. History and Topography," *AJA*, 2nd series, VIII (1904), 137-73 at 166-71. Probably Nasos also fell into Acarnanian hands with Oeniadae (see Livy xxvi. 24. 15; Polybius ix. 39. 2). The site of Nasos is uncertain; see Kirsten, col. 2209.

67. Polybius iv. 64. 4.

68. Polybius iv. 63. 10-11.

69. Polybius iv. 66. 1-2.

70. Demonstrated by Walbank, *Philip V*, pp. 40-42.

71. As even Walbank, *ibid.*, p. 41, is prepared to admit.

72. Oberhummer, p. 163, thought it likely that the Epirotes took Ambracia itself in the summer of 219; but this is probably wrong, since about 213 an Ambraciote is listed as a Delphic hieromnemon (*SIG*³, 545, l. 7), and that probably means that the city was still in Aetolian hands, cf. G. Klaffenbach, *IG*, IX², 1, p. xxix, l. 35.

73. Polybius iv. 67. 1-4; Diodorus xxvi. 7. 1. A coin of Philip probably indicates that he repaired the damage done at Dodona; see Alfred Mam-

roth, "Die Bronzemünzen des Königs Philippos V. von Makedonien," *Zeitschrift für Numismatik,* XLII (1935), 219-51, at 225, no. 4; 226-27; cf. Pl. VI, no. 4. Even so, this was far from repairing all the damage done, and the lesson for the future still held good.

74. Polybius v. 2. 1-3. Walbank, *Philip V,* p. 51, concludes that this naval policy was the result of the advice of Demetrius of Pharos, now a trusted councilor of the the king.

75. Polybius v. 3. 3. Philip had won over Scerdilaidas to his alliance in the winter of 220/19 (Polybius iv. 29. 3). The alliance was not directed against Rome (Fine, *JRS,* XXVI [1936], 37; *contra* Holleaux, *Rome,* p. 142 and n. 3). Yet this invitation to Scerdilaidas to join the allies at Cephallenia meant his breaking the treaty of 228 with Rome. But since Scerdilaidas had not been punished with Demetrius in 219, he might well reason that there was little likelihood of his being punished in 218, now that the Romans were involved with Carthage again.

76. Polybius iv. 6. 2; Walbank, *Philip V,* p. 53; see also above, p. 23.

77. Polybius v. 3. 7.

78. Polybius v. 3. 4-4. 13.

79. Polybius v. 5. 1-10. For the full implications of this decision, see Walbank, *Philip V,* p. 53.

80. Polybius first depicts the Acarnanians as being passionately anxious for revenge on the Aetolians for their many wrongs suffered at the latter people's hands. He then remarks that the Epirotes were equally eager (v. 6. 3). There may be some exaggeration in this statement, for reasons which have been outlined in connection with the campaign of 219; see above, p. 26. What the Epirotes were probably really eager for was a possible chance of additional territorial gains to augment their relatively slim pickings of the year before. Revenge on the Aetolians, particularly for the destruction of Dodona, of course also played its part.

81. Polybius v. 5. 11-14. 7.

82. Polybius v. 17. 8.

83. Polybius v. 95. 1-4, 101. 1 ff.

84. Polybius v. 96. 1-3.

85. Polybius v. 101. 3-8.

86. Polybius v. 102. 2 ff.

87. v. 101. 8-10.

88. One wonders, however, what Polybius' source for the content of a secret conversation was. It may ultimately be either court gossip, or even Polybius' own guess. J. V. A. Fine, in his review of F. W. Walbank's *Philip V, AJP,* LXIV (1943), 461-65, at 462, calls these statements of Polybius about the ambitions of Philip a "rhetorical flourish."

89. Polybius v. 101. 6-7.

90. Walbank, *Philip V,* p. 65.

91. See above, p. 17, and Niese, II, 459.

92. Polybius v. 102. 10.

93. Polybius v. 103. 7.

94. Polybius iv. 25. 6-8; cf. above, p. 24.

95. Polybius v. 104. On the authenticity of Polybius' speeches see Polybius xxxvi. 1. 7 (and the whole chapter); Hermann Ullrich, *Die Reden bei Polybios* (Zittau, 1905), esp. pp. 16, 18; Konrat Ziegler, s.v. "Polybius" No. 1, *RE*, XXI, Part 2 (Stuttgart, 1952), 1440-1578, at 1524-27, esp. 1527. Ullrich (p. 14) thinks that the figure of speech about the cloud in the west was actually used by Agelaus. Gaetano de Sanctis in his review of G. P. Landmann, *Eine Rede des Thukydides, Rivista di filologia*, LXII (1934), 108-9, thinks that Agelaus' speech is an *ex eventu* composition of Polybius. The figure was used again by the Acarnanian Lyciscus in his speech at Sparta in 211 (Polybius ix. 37. 10).

96. Polybius v. 108. It is not impossible that the Romans had instigated these activities of Scerdilaidas. See Holleaux, *Rome*, pp. 165 and n. 4, 166; idem, *CAH*, VII, 855; cf. Livy xxii. 33. 5.

97. Fine, *JRS*, XXVI (1936), 26-28, and map, p. 27; cf. Zippel, p. 63; Holleaux, *Rome*, p. 167.

98. Walbank, *Philip V*, p. 69.

99. Polybius v. 109-10.

100. Polybius v. 110. 10-11.

101. vii. 9. The version given by Livy (xxiii. 33. 10-12; cf. Zonaras ix. 4. 2) may be disregarded as an obvious annalistic fabrication. See, *e.g.*, J. Kromayer, "Hannibal als Staatsmann," *Historische Zeitschrift*, CIII (1909), 237-73, at 244-46.

102. Polybius vii. 9. 13.

103. Polybius vii. 9. 1, 5, 7; 9. 1 expressly says that the ambassador is acting in the name of "the allies" as well as of Philip and the Macedonians.

104. See above, p. 19.

105. In 215 Aratus is reported to have told Philip that the Acarnanians and other peoples obey the king's commands (Plutarch *Aratus* 50). The Epirotes are not mentioned, but this signifies little, for Aratus is merely enumerating to Philip the various peoples who are devoted to him, to whom he is the "darling" of Greece.

106. Polybius ix. 38. 5, xi. 5. 4.

107. Livy xxix. 12. 8.

108. Livy xxvi. 25. 11; cf. Polybius ix. 40. 6.

109. With the exception of a passage in Silius Italicus (*Punica* xv. 296 ff.). Silius has almost certainly confused the Social with the First Macedonian Was as the passage itself clearly shows, and his account may safely be disregarded; cf. Oberhummer, p. 170, n. 2.

110. So Holleaux, *Rome*, p. 214, n. 2; Täubler, p. 218, and n. 3; *contra* Niese, II, 477, n. 3 (by implication); De Sanctis, *Storia*, III, Part 2, 435, n. 91 (largely on the basis of Polybius xi. 5. 4).

111. Holleaux, *Rome*, p. 214, n. 2.

112. Livy xxvi. 24. 11. On the interpretation of this clause, see the works cited below, n. 130.

113. Livy xxix. 12. 14; Walbank, *Philip V*, p. 86, n. 6.

114. See above, p. 25.

115. And probably soon after the treaty, for Epirus was neutral in the late summer or early autumn of 211, when the Acarnanians sent their non-

combatants to Epirus (see below, p. 35). Aetolian attacks on Epirus in the past had not been uncommon; the Aetolian land hunger was notorious; and Aetolia now had a powerful ally in what might prove to be a general Hellenic war. These or similar considerations might have led the Epirotes to try to remain aloof from the conflict which was about to begin.

116. So, of course, Holleaux, *Rome,* pp. 178 ff.
117. Livy xxiii. 38. 7-10; Polybius viii. 1. 6; cf. Holleaux, *Rome,* p. 187, n. 1, for the correction of Livy's fifty-five ships to fifty.
118. Livy xxiii. 38. 9.
119. Livy xxiv. 40; cf. Walbank, *Philip V,* pp. 75-76 and nn.; Holleaux, "Rome and Macedon: Philip against the Romans," "Rome and Macedon: The Romans against Philip," "Rome and Antiochus," *CAH,* VIII (Cambridge [England], 1930), 116-240, at 122; *idem, Rome,* p. 192.
120. See above, pp. 29, 31
121. Livy xxiv. 40. 7.
122. On the importance of the coastal cities, see Livy xxiv. 40. 4; for Atintania, *ibid.,* xxvii. 30. 13, xxix. 12. 13; and in general see Fine, *JRS,* XXVI (1936), 31; Niese, II, 474.
123. On the potential importance of Tarentum for Philip, see Livy xxiv. 13. 5; cf. J. H. Thiel, *Studies on the History of Roman Sea-Power in Republican Times* (Amsterdam, 1946), p. 100.
124. See now the discussion in Walbank, *Philip V,* pp. 81-82. Walbank concludes that it is not likely Philip would have made such an attempt.
125. I am following Livy's chronology and placing the alliance with Aetolia in 211 B.C. This presents certain difficulties, which are not insuperable, however; and until we have something like a certain list of the Aetolian *strategoi* in the last two decades of the third century B.C., any revision of 211 B.C. to 212 B.C. on the basis of the order of that list is certainly clarifying *minime obscura per obscuriora* (cf. Klaffenbach, *IG,* IX², 1, p. xlix). See the excellent and convincing discussion of the chronological problems involved in Walbank, *Philip V,* pp. 301-4, with nn. for citations of earlier discussions. Walbank settles on 211 B.C.
126. Polybius v. 107. 5-7; Walbank, *Philip V,* p. 82 and nn. 3-4.
127. Livy xxv. 23. 8-9 (which shows that the negotiations were begun in 212), xxvi. 24. 1.
128. Livy xxvi. 24. 6, 8.
129. Cf. Oberhummer, p. 167, n. 1.
130. Livy xxvi. 24. 9-15. For the interpretation of the Corcyra clause see Larsen, *Economic Survey,* IV, 264; Holleaux, *Rome,* 214, n. 2; Walbank, *Philip V,* p. 84.
131. See Holleaux, *Rome,* p. 217 and *passim.*
132. Perhaps one of the nearby Echinades islands; see above, p. 26 and n. 66.
133. Livy xxvi. 24. 15; cf. Polybius ix. 39. 2.
134. Livy xxvi. 25; cf. Polybius ix. 40. 4-6, xvi. 32. 3.
135. See Polybius ix. 28-31 for the speech of the Aetolian Chlaeneas; ix. 32-39 for Lyciscus' speech.
136. Polybius ix. 37. 5-7, 10, 38. 9, 39. 1-4. On the validity of the speeches

in Polybius, see above, n. 95; for the speech of Lyciscus see also Holleaux, *Rome*, p. 18 and nn. 2-3.

137. Polybius x. 41. 1, 3, 8; Livy xxviii. 5. 4-5, 9.
138. Polybius x. 41. 4. In a compressed and confused passage Appian (*Macedonica* 3. 1) says that the Aetolians with Roman help (Appian implies in 205 B.C., when the Aetolians had already made peace!) took Ambracia (implying that it was Epirote) and lost it almost at once. This is clearly an annalistic fabrication; see Salvetti, *Studi di storia antica*, II (1893), 120; Giuseppe Clementi, "La guerra annibalica in oriente," *ibid.*, I (1891), 51-79, at 77; so Holleaux, *Rome*, p. 245, n. 2; Walbank, *Philip V*, p. 99, n. 9.
139. Livy xxix. 12. 1.
140. Niese, II, 494.
141. Holleaux, *CAH*, VIII, 132; *idem*, *Rome*, pp. 247, 244, n. 2; *contra* Thiel, p. 131.
142. De Sanctis, *Storia*, III, Part 2, 429.
143. Livy xxxii. 21. 17; cf. Holleaux, *Rome*, p. 254.
144. Livy xxix. 12. 1.
145. Polybius xviii. 38. 8; and cf. the whole course of later events. Heuss, p. 39, followed by Karl-Ernst Petzold, *Die Eröffnung des zweiten römisch-makedonischen Krieges. Untersuchungen zur spätannalistischen Topik bei Livius* (Berlin, 1940), p. 14 and n. 14, holds that the treaty was not permanent and would expire at the end of the war anyway; *contra*, Larsen, *CP*, XXX (1935), 212.
146. Since they were compelled to cede Oeniadae to the Acarnanians in 189 (Polybius xxi. 32. 14; Livy xxxviii. 11. 9). On the treaty as a whole and what may be inferred about its provisions see Walbank, *Philip V*, p. 100, n. 1; Holleaux, *CAH*, VIII, 134-35.
147. Livy xxix. 12. 2; cf. the garbled account in Appian *Macedonica* 3. 1.
148. So De Sanctis, *Storia*, III, Part 2, 432; cf. Holleaux, *Rome*, pp. 284-86; *idem*, *CAH*, VIII, 135. Holleaux, of course, maintains that Rome's resumption of the offensive was essentially defensive.
149. By J. A. O. Larsen, "The Peace of Phoenice and the Outbreak of the Second Macedonian War," *CP*, XXXII (1937), 15-31, at 31, n. 48; cf. Petzold, p. 25.
150. Cf. Livy xxix. 12. 2, 12. 16.
151. Livy xxix. 12. 5.
152. Livy xxix. 12. 3, 5.
153. I shall here avoid as much as possible the controversy over this *pax communis*. It is probable, however, that *communis* refers simply to the Romans, Philip, and the Epirotes (for this use of "communis" see Livy xxix. 11. 2). A peace between the Romans and Philip must include the Epirotes; it would end their ambiguous relationship both to Philip and the Romans. Hence *pax communis* is not necessarily a translation of κοινὴ εἰρήνη as Elias Bickermann, "Les préliminaires de la seconde guerre de Macédoine," *Revue de philologie, de littérature et d'histoire anciennes*, LXI (1935), 59-81, 161-76, will have it. *Contra* Bickermann: Larsen, *CP*. XXXII (1937), 15-31; A. H. McDonald and F. W. Walbank,

"The Origins of the Second Macedonian War," *JRS*, XXVII (1937), 180-207; Petzold, pp. 23-24.

154. Livy xxix. 12. 8-12.
155. So Heinrich Nissen, *Kritische Untersuchungen über die Quellen der vierten und fünften Dekade des Livius* (Berlin, 1863), pp. 84-85; and cf. Holleaux, *Rome*, p. 258, n. 4; *idem*, "Études d'histoire hellénistique. XI. Le prétendu recours des Athéniens aux Romains en 201/200," *REA*, XXII (1920), 77-96, at 94, n. 4; Petzold, p. 11.
156. Others of the allies were "ab rege foederi adscripti." Possibly this means they signed the treaty (so Walbank, *Philip V*, p. 103). If so, they might have been present at Phoenice. Yet the special mention of Epirotes and Acarnanians suggests that these were the only allies represented.
157. Livy xxix. 12. 12.
158. So De Sanctis, *Storia*, III, Part 2, 435-36; Holleaux, *Rome*, p. 278, n. 2, followed by Walbank, *Philip V*, p. 103. Cf. Polybius xviii. 1. 14. Atintania alone is specifically mentioned by Livy as given to Philip (xxix. 12. 13).
159. Livy xxvii. 30. 13; on Rome behind these demands, see Walbank, *Philip V*, p. 90.
160. (P?) xxix. 12. 13.
161. The list of those included by the Romans in particular, and the meaning of "foederi adscripti," have been the subject of much inconclusive debate. See the articles cited above, n. 153; further discussions are cited by Walbank, *Philip V*, p. 103, n. 6, with a summary of the various views. For a new meaning of "foederi adscripti," add to Walbank's list, Petzold, pp. 17-23.
162. Larsen, *CP*, XXX (1935), 195.
163. xxix. 12. 14.
164. On the other hand, as far as we know, the *hegemon* of the Hellenic League had no power to make a treaty binding on the league without the league's consent, as Bickermann, *Revue de philologie, de littérature et d'histoire anciennes*, LXI (1935), 65, points out. We know little or nothing about the history of these years except as it affects Rome. One could conjecture that Philip had been empowered by the Hellenic League to act for it (as in 215 with Hannibal; see above, p. 30). It is by no means impossible that in 206, upon the occasion of the peace with Aetolia, Philip had been empowered to make peace with Rome also, whenever he could secure equitable conditions. In 205 Philip was desirous of making peace with the Romans, if possible, as he had with the Aetolians, even before the Epirotes broached the subject (Livy xxix. 12. 7). That the Epirotes approached the Romans first, then Philip, harmonizes with the belief that they already knew that Philip was agreeable. True, in 205 Philip did some campaigning against the Romans (Livy xxix. 12. 5); but he had seized Zacynthus in 217 when the negotiations to end the Social War had already begun (Polybius v. 102. 10). The foregoing is pure conjecture, but it shows that the objection of Bickermann is not insuperable.
165. Heuss, pp. 12-13; cf. Pomponius *Digest* xlix. 15. 5. 2.
166. If Petzold (pp. 18-19) be right in arguing that the "ab Romanis foederi adscripti" did not by virtue of that fact obtain a treaty with Rome, then *a fortiori* the "ab rege foederi adscripti" didn't.

167. Eventually the Romans chose to regard Acarnanian participation in the Second Macedonian War as a breach of *amicitia* with Rome; cf. Livy xlii. 38. 3-4; below, p. 71.
168. Livy xxxiii. 16. 2.
169. Ernest Kirsten, "Die albanische Frage des Altertums," *Die Welt als Geschichte. Eine Zeitschrift für Universalgeschichte*, VIII (1942), 75-96, at 86-87.
170. In general see Holleaux, *Rome*, pp. 271-72.

Chapter III

1. See Larsen, *CP*, XXX (1935), 193-214, esp. 204-5; and *idem*, *Economic Survey*, IV, 286-90, for an impressive list of Roman embassies to Greece and other kinds of supervisory interference in the early second century. See also Rostovtzeff, I, 56-57; II, 1016-17; André Aymard, *Les premiers rapports de Rome et de la Confédération achaienne (198-189 avant J.C.)* (Bordeaux, 1938). A.N. Sherwin-White, *The Roman Citizenship* (Oxford, 1939), pp. 151-52, puts it very succinctly: "The Roman adaptation of the declaration of freedom thus preserved the rights of conquest, without involving Rome in the encumbrance of provincial government." Holleaux, *CAH*, VIII, 239-40, had foreshadowed the development of this interpretation, for he pointed out that the "freedom" of Greece after 196 was of a decidedly peculiar variety; cf. *ibid.*, p. 195.
2. Polybius xviii. 44, 46. 5; cf. Larsen, *Economic Survey*, IV, 274.
3. Polybius xvi. 27. 2-3, 34; Livy xxxi. 18. 1-3; Diodorus xxviii. 6; cf. Larsen, *CP*, XXX (1935), 204-5.
4. *CAH*, VIII, 239; cf. *idem*, *Rome*, pp. 329-30. Holleaux's view has been restated with modifications by A. H. McDonald, *JRS*, XXVII (1937), 205-7; cf. 180, n. 1. For the view that the Second Macedonian War represented imperialism, see Gaetano de Sanctis, *Storia*, IV, Part 1, 21-28; *idem*, "Dopoguerra antico," *Atene e Roma*, n.s., I (1920), 3-14, 73-89, at 81-82. De Sanctis, *Atene e Roma, ibid.*; *idem*, *Storia*, IV, Part 1, 576; *idem*, Review of R. M. Haywood's *Studies on Scipio Africanus*, *Rivista di filologia*, LXIV (1936), 189-203, at 196; and Jérome Carcopino, *Points de vue sur l'imperialisme romain* (Paris, 1934), pp. 10-11, 67-68; and others see behind this imperialism the hand of Scipio Africanus. It is difficult to avoid the conclusion that, if Roman foreign policy took a new departure in the years after 205, it was Africanus, Rome's most powerful general, statesman, and party leader, who was responsible. On the preeminence of Scipio, see Friederich Münzer, *Römische Adelsparteien und Adelsfamilien* (Stuttgart, 1920), p. 91; and, with exaggerations, Werner Schur, *Scipio Africanus und die Begründung der römischen Weltherrschaft* (Leipzig, 1927).
5. *CAH*, VIII, 149 ff.; *Rome*, pp. 306 ff.
6. David Magie, "The 'Agreement' Between Philip V and Antiochus III for the partition of the Egyptian Empire," *JRS*, XXIX (1939), 32-44, thinks that the compact never really existed, that it was a myth trumped up by the Rhodians and Attalus to frighten Rome. Howsoever that may be,

since the Romans believed in the existence of such an agreement, as Magie himself admits, its reality is immaterial to the present purpose.

7. Livy xxxi. 29. 4, xxx. 26. 2; Appian *Macedonica* 4. 2; cf. Holleaux, *Rome*, p. 293, n. 1.

8. Some variants upon this reconstruction have been advanced in recent years. Alfredo Passerini, "Studi di storia ellenistico-romana. II. I moventi di Roma nella seconda guerra macedonica," *Athenaeum*, IX (1931), 542-62, at 548-51, sought to show that it was fear of Philip rather than fear of the alliance between Macedonia and Antiochus which led Rome to go to war (criticized by De Sanctis, *Rivista di filologia*, LXIV [1936], 198-99 and 199, n. 1). G. T. Griffith, "An Early Motive of Roman Imperialism (201 B.C.)," *Cambridge Historical Journal*, V (1935), 1-14, accepts Holleaux in the main, but adds an important secondary motive: Rome's fear of the new Macedonian fleet which Philip had constructed and which had won several victories in the east. Elias Bickermann, *Revue de philologie, de littérature et d'histoire anciennes*, LXI (1935), 59-81, regarding the Peace of Phoenice as a κοινὴ εἰρήνη thinks that Rome went unwillingly to war because of the obligations she had undertaken as a guarantor of that treaty. M. A. Levi, *La politica imperiale di Roma* (2nd ed.; Turin, 1936), pp. 106-17, has recently revived the old theory that the basic motive of Roman imperialism was economic, but this idea has been refuted satisfactorily long ago and many times; see Tenney Frank, *Roman Imperialism*, pp. 276 ff.; idem, "Mercantilism and Rome's Foreign Policy," *AHR*, XVIII (1912-13), 233-52; Hatzfeld, pp. 369-76; Holleaux, *Rome*, pp. 83-93. At least so far as the immediate circumstances of the outbreak of the Second Macedonian War are concerned, Holleaux still seems best; so Walbank, *Philip V*, p. 128.

9. Livy xxxi. 4. 4, 5. 1, 6. 1; cf. Polybius xvi. 24. 1-2. The sending of Laevinus to the east in 201 B.C. to keep an eye on Philip is an obvious annalistic fabrication (Livy xxxi. 3. 2 ff.), a duplication from the First Macedonian War. See Petzold, pp. 72, 77 ff. The historicity of this mission is, nevertheless, defended by Thiel, pp. 219-23.

10. Polyaenus iv. 18. 2.

11. Cf. Livy xxxii. 14. 5.

12. Cf. Livy xxxiii. 16. 5.

13. Polybius xv. 22.

14. On unrest in the league generally, see Holleaux, *Rome*, pp. 224-30. On Philip's mistakes in policy and his outraging of Greek public opinion, see Walbank, *Philip V*, pp. 135-37, 272.

15. Livy xxxi. 14. 9.

16. De Sanctis, *Storia*, IV, Part 1, 19, n. 51, cites Isocrates xvi *(De bigis)*. 6, for Athenian attitude toward the mysteries.

17. Livy xxxi. 14. 6-10. The chronology of this Acarnanian-Athenian-Macedonian imbroglio has given rise to a considerable amount of discussion. The raid on Attica has regularly been considered the cause of the abolition of the Athenian tribes Antigonis and Demetrias, named in honor of the founders of the Antigonid house. W. S. Ferguson, *Hellenistic Athens* (London, 1911), p. 268 and n. 4, argued that the only likely occasion for the abolition of these tribes was in 201 B.C. when the order of the

secretary cycle was broken. Hence the raid on Athens also occurred in 201 B.C. Later, Ferguson, in *Athenian Tribal Cycles in the Hellenistic Age* (Cambridge [Massachusetts], 1932), p. 141, n. 1, argued that the raid could have occurred while Philip was still absent in Asia; *i.e,* Philip could have ordered it from Greece. Ferguson thought that the mysteries profaned were those of Boedromion (September), 201 B.C., and that the raid happened later in the fall (so Bickermann, *Revue de philologie, de littérature et d'histoire anciennes,* LXI [1935], 164, n. 3 *ad fin*). Recently, however, McDonald, *JRS,* XXVI (1937), 191, has shown that there is reason to connect the abolition of the tribes with anti-Macedonian sentiment at Athens before the raid (cf. Petzold, p. 33, n. 12); indeed, probably one of the reasons for Philip's agreement to participate in the raid was his resentment at Athens' anti-Macedonian attitude. Against Philip's ordering of the raid from Bargylia, Walbank, *Philip V,* pp. 311-12, argues that Philip was probably held there incommunicado by his enemies' blockade. W. B. Dinsmoor, *The Athenian Archon List in the Light of Recent Discoveries* (New York, 1939), pp. 172-73, reexamines all the arguments, including the technical ones from the cycles of Athenian magistrates and tribes. He accepts McDonald's reasoning that the provocation for the abolition of Antigonis and Demetrias was not the raid on Attica, and concludes that the two tribes were abolished in the spring of 201. Hence Philip's raid could fall in the spring of 200 as Holleaux, *CAH,* VIII, 161 (followed by Walbank, *ibid.*), had argued. The mysteries profaned, then, were those of Boedromion (August/September), 201. W. K. Pritchett and B. D. Meritt, *The Chronology of Hellenistic Athens* (Cambridge [Mass.], 1940), p. 109, follow Dinsmoor and McDonald in dating the rupture of relations between Athens and Macedonia and the abolition of the tribes to spring-summer, 201 B.C. Cf. also Pritchett's dissertation, *The Five Attic Tribes After Kleisthenes* (Baltimore, 1943), p. 33. Silvio Accame, "Una lettera di Filippo V e i primordi della seconda guerra macedonica," *Rivista di filologia,* LXIX (1942), 179-93, at 187-88 rejects this dating. His arguments, however, do not fully refute the epigraphical arguments on the other side. Accame (pp. 179-80) publishes an inscription (a letter of Philip V) which he interprets as showing the odium which the Greek world felt for the impiety of Philip after his (effective) consent to the Acarnanian profanation of the Eleusinian mysteries.

18. Livy xxxi. 15. 5.
19. Polybius xvi. 25-26; Livy xxxi. 15. 1-8. The annalistic view that the Second Macedonian War was begun by the Romans to protect the Athenians from Philip as a result of an Athenian appeal to Rome (cf. Livy xxxi. 1. 9-10), whether as fact or as Roman pretext, has been disproved by Maurice Holleaux, "Études d'histoire hellénistique. XI. Le prétendu recours des Athéniens aux Romains en 201/200," *REA,* XXII (1920), 77-96; *contra,* De Sanctis, *Storia,* IV, Part 1, 32, n. 65; Bickermann, *Revue de philologie, de litterature et d'histoire anciennes,* LXI (1935), 164. The opposing arguments of Holleaux and De Sanctis are conveniently summarized by H. H. Scullard, *A History of the Roman World From 753 to 146 B.C.* (1st ed.; New York, 1939), pp. 463-64; cf. 2nd ed. (London, 1951), pp. 432-33. For recent defenses of Holleaux's main thesis, see Petzold, pp. 66-81; Larsen, *CP,* XXXII (1937), 15-31; McDonald, *JRS,* XXVII (1937), 180-207. Accame, *Rivista di filologia,*

LXIX (1942), 183-85, however, has once again argued that the embassies of Athens played a part in bringing about the war.
20. Livy xxxi. 6. 1, 3, cf. 5. 2-3. According to Livy (*ibid.*, 7-8.1), almost immediately thereafter Sulpicius summoned a *contio* and harangued the people to such good effect that the declaration of war passed the *comitia*. This chronology is almost certainly wrong: the unsuccessful measure was voted on at the opening of the year; the war was not approved until summer (July?); see Holleaux, *CAH*, VIII, 164, and nn. 1 and 2; Walbank, *Philip V*, pp. 314-15.
21. Polybius xvi. 27. 5; Livy xxxi. 2. 3-4; Appian *Macedonica* 4. 2.
22. So Walbank, *Philip V*, pp. 313-14 (with references); for chronology, see *ibid*.
23. Polybius xvi. 27. 2.
24. Frank, *Roman Imperialism*, p. 161, n. 29, says that this is less than Flamininus demanded in 198 (see below, pp. 46-47, 49). Rather, it is only a difference in phrasing. In 198 Flamininus demanded that Philip withdraw his garrisons from the states of Greece. But this is implied in 200. If Philip could make war on no Greek state, obviously he could keep garrisons in no Greek state; for in an attempt of cities garrisoned by Philip to expell the garrisons, according to the strict letter of the ultimatum, the garrisons could not defend themselves — which is absurd. Besides, the garrisons would be useless if Philip could make war on no Greek state. The famous "fetters of Greece" held the country in submission out of fear of armed force from those centers. If Philip could not use such armed force, maintaining the garrisons would be useless. H. H. Scullard, *Roman politics 220-150 B.C.* (Oxford, 1951), p. 102, follows Frank.
25. Xenophon *Hellenica* v. 1. 31. Cf. Täubler, p. 43; James S. Reid, *The Municipalities of the Roman Empire* (Cambridge [England], 1913), p. 23, seems to regard the policy as of native Roman origin, but he is probably wrong.
26. Polybius ix. 28-31 (the speech of Chlaeneas to the Lacedaemonians); cf. Livy (P) xxxi. 15. 10-11. Legal justification for this proclamation of Greek liberty there was none; cf. Petzold, p. 37, n. 32: "Man masste sich einfach dieses Recht an, ohne sich auf irgendeine juristische Grundlage stellen zu können oder überhaupt zu stellen.... Das gleiche Verfahren wurde auch Nabis und Antiochos gegenüber erfolgreich angewandt."
27. See above, pp. 10-11
28. Polybius xvi. 27. 4.
29. Aymard, *Premiers rapports*, p. 139, n. 25, explains the omission of a visit to Sparta, Elis, and Messene on the ground that these states were too far from the center of things at that time to be useful against Philip.
30. Cf. Holleaux, *Rome*, p. 307, n. 1.
31. Livy xxxii. 14. 5.
32. There is no trace of Philip's having summoned the *synedrion* of the Hellenic League to back him in the impending struggle with Rome. The Eastern War had been a war of conquest for Macedonia, in the initiation of which the *synedrion* had not been consulted; the allies might well regard the Roman war as simply a new phase of the Eastern War. Moreover, the

Achaeans, the most important of the allies, were the friends of Egypt and Rhodes. See the discussion of De Sanctis, *Storia,* IV, Part 1, 40-41.

33. Polybius xvi. 27. 1-3, 4, 34. 1-7; Livy xxxi. 18. 1-5; Diodorus xxviii. 6. In the interpretation, interrelation, and chronology of these events I have followed Walbank, *Philip V,* pp. 314-16; see also McDonald, *JRS,* XXVII (1937), 180-207; Petzold, p. 42 and n. 58.

34. For the technical questions of the fetial procedure involved, see Walbank, *JRS,* XXVII (1937), 192-97. Walbank further defended his views in "Roman Declaration of War in the Third and Second Centuries," *CP,* XLIV (1949), 15-19, esp. 17-19, against Elias Bickermann, *"Bellum Philippicum:* Some Greek and Roman Views Concerning the Causes of the Second Macedonian War," *CP,* XL (1945), 137-48, at 139.

35. Livy xxxi. 14. 2, 22. 4-5, 27. 1.

36. Livy xxxi. 28. 1-4.

37. Livy xxxi. 18. 9, remarks, "nuntii occurrerunt consulem iam in Epiro esse et Apolloniam terrestres copias navales Corcyram deduxisse"; but unfortunately Livy seems to have thought that Apollonia was in Epirus (cf. xxxv. 24. 7, xlii. 18. 3, 36. 8). Hence he may well have made this mistake here.

38. Livy xxxi. 40. 9-10, cf. 36. 6 ff.

39. De Sanctis, *Storia,* IV, Part 1, 58-59.

40. Livy xxxii. 5. 9, says that Philip's destination was Chaonia, but he is speaking vaguely. Chaonia is on the coast; Atintania is inland in the valley of the river Aous around Antigoneia, near which the battle was fought (Livy xxxii. 5. 9). For the geographical location of ancient Atintania, see Scylax Caryandensis 26; Nilsson, *Lunds Universitets Arsskrift,* N. F. Afd. 1, VI, No. 4 (1909), 55-56; Hans Treidler, *Epirus im Altertum. Studien zur historischen Topographie* (Liepzig, 1917), pp. 81-85; Holleaux, *Rome,* p. 106; for the discussions concerning the exact site, see Walbank, *Philip V,* p. 149, n. 1 and references. Whether the battle of the Aous occurred technically in Atintania (Macedonian soil) or in Epirus is difficult to determine. It was near Antigoneia, however, and that was in Atintania. Although De Sanctis, *Storia,* IV, Part 1, 60, n. 117, puts the battle much nearer Antigoneia than Walbank does, he holds that fighting the battle there violated Epirote neutrality. Since the battle was fought in a pass regularly known as "the pass of Epirus," or "the pass by Epirus," it probably occurred approximately on the Epirote-Atintanian boundary (for citations of the name applied to the pass, see Walbank, *ibid.*). It is quite likely, as Walbank suggests, that Polybius had no very clear idea of the geography of the battle site. Plutarch, *Flamininus* 3, is wrong when he says the Apsus instead of the Aous.

41. De Sanctis, *Storia,* IV, Part 1, 59.

42. Livy xxxii. 6. 1. On Charops as an oligarch, see Polybius xxvii. 15. 2; Livy xxxii. 11. 1; Plutarch *Flamininus* 4.

43. Livy xxxii. 3. 2-7.

44. Livy xxxii. 6. 1-4, 9. 1, 6; Plutarch *Flamininus* 3. Hence the statement in Livy xxxii. 28. 6, that Flamininus had been detained at Rome for the greater part of the year, must either be false or a gross exaggeration.

45. Livy xxxii. 9. 6-8.
46. Livy xxxii. 9. 8-10.1; minor attacks and skirmishes: Plutarch *Flamininus* 4.
47. Livy xxxii. 10. 1-8; Diodorus xxviii. 11; Appian *Macedonica* 5. Léon Homo, "Flamininus et la politique romaine en Grèce (198-194 av. J.-C.)," *Revue historique,* CXXI (1916), 241-79; CXXII (1916), 1-32; at CXXI, 243, suggests as a possible motive for Philip's seeking this conference his fear that the Epirotes might have been engaged in secret negotiations with the Romans and that they might show the latter how to turn his position.
48. "Ita crederet, ut suae potius omnia quam illius potestatis essent" (Livy xxxii. 11. 4).
49. Polybius xxvii. 15. 2; Livy xxxii. 10. 9-11. 6. Plutarch *Flamininus* 4, tells the same story with some differences of detail. Most importantly Plutarch implies that there were several shepherds, not just one, and that they brought Charops himself with them to the Roman camp as surety of their good faith. Livy's version seems the more plausible, since the good faith of Charops had already been shown by his dealings with Villius, which Plutarch omits. Plutarch also says that the guides were kept in chains as they led the way. This might be true. Cf. also: Ennius *Annales* 335-8 (V³) *apud* Cicero *De Senectute* 1 (Ennius seems to imply that the shepherd expected a reward, as seems very likely); Diodorus xxx. 5; Appian *Macedonica* 6; *De viris illustribus* 51. 1.
50. Livy xxxii. 11. 6-12. 10.
51. Livy xxxii. 14. 7.
52. Livy xxxii. 15. 5-6.
53. Cf. Livy xxxiii. 16-17.
54. Cf. Livy xxxii. 15. 5.
55. Cf. Livy xxxiii. 16. 3.
56. Livy xxxii. 14. 5, 8.
57. Contrast the treatment meted out to Phaloria in Thessaly after Flamininus had left Epirus. The town was burned and destroyed as an example to the rest of Thessaly, despite the fact that the chief resistance had come from a Macedonian garrison of 2,000 in the place (Livy xxxii. 15. 1-3).
58. Livy xxxii. 14. 6, 15. 5; Plutarch *Flamininus* 5. 1-2. (Walbank, *Philip V,* p. 156, n. 1, cites Plutarch *Flamininus* 5. 2, for Roman restraint in Epirus, but remarks that the passage is not clearly relevant. 5.1 and 3, do show clearly that Epirus is meant.)
59. Niese, II, 612; Fritz Geyer, *s.v.* "Philippos" (10), *RE,* XIX (1937-38), cols. 2303-31, at 2320. De Sanctis, *Storia,* IV, Part 1, 60, n. 117, holds that the battle of the Aous was on Epirote territory and thinks, therefore, that Epirote neutrality was not observed. But it is impossible to determine the site of the battle more accurately than that it took place near the boundary of Macedonian Atintania and Epirus. In any case, even if the battle did take place in Epirus (cf. Polybius xviii. 23. 4, where the language should not be pressed to the hilt for a few miles one way or another, and note that Polybius' knowledge of the details of the geography of this area was very vague), the violation of neutrality was a technical one.

60. Walbank, *Philip V*, p. 319.
61. Livy xxxii. 14. 7.
62. Livy xxxii. 32. 6-9. For analyses of the diplomacy involved, see Maurice Holleaux, "Études d'histoire hellénistique. Les conférences de Lokride et la politique de T. Quinctius Flamininus," *REG*, XXXVI (1923), 115-71; Aymard, *Premiers rapports*, pp. 114-27. The objections raised to Holleaux's thesis by Frederic M. Wood, "The Tradition of Flamininus' 'Selfish Ambition' in Polybius and Later Historians," *TAPA*, LXX (1939), 93-103, are not convincing.
63. Livy xxxii. 32. 9.
64. Polybius xviii. 1. 13-14; cf. Livy xxxii. 33. 3. On the proper interpretation of these passages see Holleaux, *Rome*, p. 278, n. 1; Zippel, p. 73.
65. See above, p. 37.
66. Polybius xviii. 9. 1; cf. Livy xxxii. 35. 12.
67. Polybius xviii. 10. 1-12. 14; cf. Livy xxxii. 36. 6-37. 6. For the prorogation of Flamininus' command, see Livy xxxii. 28. 9.
68. Holleaux, *CAH*, VIII, 173.
69. Cf. Livy xxxiii. 14. 5
70. Livy xxxii. 18. 3.
71. Livy xxxiii. 1-2.
72. Livy xxxii. 40. 7.
73. Livy xxxiii. 16.
74. Livy xxxiii. 17.
75. Livy xxxiii. 17. 15; the epitomator of book xxxiii says Lucius "Acarnanas . . . in deditionem accepit."
76. Täubler, p. 16 and n. 3.
77. Livy xxxiii. 16. 1; cf. *ILS*, 14. This inscription mentions only the capture of Leucas and says nothing of the surrender of Acarnania, but it would be unsafe to attempt to draw any conclusions from the omission.
78. Polybius xviii. 38. 2; cf. Livy xxxiii. 13. 4.
79. Polybius xviii. 7. 7.
80. Polybius xviii. 42. 4; cf. Livy xxxiii. 25. 6-7.
81. J. A. O. Larsen, "The Treaty of Peace at the Conclusion of the Second Macedonian War," *CP*, XXXI (1936), 342-48.
82. See above, p. 49.
83. Holleaux, *CAH*, VIII, 177; cf. Polybius xviii. 37. 10, and the very wording of the Isthmian proclamation of 196 (Polybius xviii. 46. 5): "The Roman Senate and Titus Quintius . . . , having overcome King Philip and the Macedonians . . . "
84. After the time of the Brachylles murder affair, which occurred in winter (Livy xxxiii. 30. 1 [cf. Polybius xviii. 44. 1], 27.5); and presumably at the opening of the sailing season.
85. Polybius xviii. 44; Livy xxxiii. 30 (with additions usually rejected, cf. Nissen, pp. 144-48; Maurice Holleaux, "Notes sur Tite-Live. I. Les additions annalistiques au traité de 196 (33, 30, 6-11)," *Revue de philologie, de littérature et d'histoire anciennes*, LVII [1931], 5-19; Petzold, pp. 92 ff. Petzold still wrongly calls the document a treaty.).

86. Polybius xviii. 44. 2-3 (Paton's translation in the Loeb Library).
87. Polybius xviii. 45. 1-6; cf. Livy xxxiii. 31. 1-3.
88. Polybius xviii. 45. 7-12; cf. Livy xxxiii. 31. 7-11.
89. Beloch, I, Part 2, 146 ff.
90. Polybius xviii. 46. 5 (Paton's translation in the Loeb Library); cf. Livy xxxiii. 32. 5; Plutarch *Flamininus* 10; Appian *Macedonica* 9. 4; Valerius Maximus iv. 8. 5.
91 Technically, of course, Acarnania was not a place which Philip had surrendered to the Romans; the Acarnanians had surrendered themselves, but the important consideration is that they had surrendered to Rome, and were thus in the same condition as the places which Philip had surrendered, as far as Roman control was concerned.
92. The omission of Acarnania from the proclamation does not mean that the Aetolians would have protested this particular point. They had designs on Leucas themselves; see below, p. 54. On the other hand they were quite capable of complaining of Roman designs on a place they desired for themselves. The silence of Polybius both about Aetolian rumors regarding Acarnania and about Roman discussions of that country is not decisive, for there is no reason to suppose that the historian has seen fit to mention all the rumors or all the points of Flamininus' discussion of them with the commissioners, or even to assume that Polybius' information on these points was complete.
93. Cf. Oberhummer, pp. 177-78.
94. Livy xxxiv. 26. 11.
95. Cf. Heuss, pp. 112-13: "In gleicher Weise besteht die Möglichkeit dass die dedierte Gemeinde durch Zurückziehung der römischen Herrschaft wieder ihre staatliche Unabhängigkeit gewinnt, und sich dann in Verhältniss zu Rom der völkerrechtliche Freundschaftzustand herstellt." And as Larsen *(CP,* XXX [1935], 197-98) points out, deditio might be followed by treatment even more favorable than the granting of a treaty. Eusebius *Chronikon,* p. 115 (Karst), is the only reference to a grant of freedom to the Acarnanians, the Epirotes being coupled with them. It has almost no value as evidence, of course. On the general meaning of *deditio,* see also above, p. 13.
96. See above, p. 34.
97. Polybius xviii. 47. 8-9; Livy xxxiii. 34. 7. If this is anything more than a merry-go-round on which the Aetolians were ironically invited to embark, it may imply that the disposition of Leucas and Acarnania was an act of Flamininus confirmed by a blanket validation of the senate which did not mention Leucas (Acarnania) specifically.
98. Livy xxxiii. 49. 8.
99. Oberhummer, p. 177. Alfredo Passerini, "Studi di storia ellenistico-romana. III. La pace con Filippo e le relazioni con Antioco," *Athenaeum,* X (1932), 105-26, at 114, n. 4, thinks that Aetolian emphasis on acquiring Pharsalus and Echinus (which the Aetolians also wanted) in their appeals to Flamininus and the senate shows that Leucas ought to have been given them, *i.e.,* they fully expected it to be. But one cannot be sure that the brief notices in the sources correctly represent the relative emphasis which the Aetolians placed on their pleas for these places. Nor, even assuming that the sources correctly represent this matter, does Passerini's conclusion necessarily follow. The Aetolians might very well have attached more importance to the acquisition of Pharsalus and Echinus.
100. Dionysius Halicarnassensis i. 51. 2 (the mention of Anactorium in this connection is an obvious mistake); see also below, appendix, pp. 92-97.

101. So Larsen, *Economic Survey*, IV, 275-76.
102. Cf. Holleaux, *CAH*, VIII, 183.
103. Cf. Larsen, *CP*, XXX (1935), 201-2. As Larsen points out, while Heuss (pp. 84 ff.; cf. Aymard, *Premiers rapports*, pp. 273 ff.) is right in denying Täubler's (pp. 228 ff., 432 ff., 437-38) theory that Rome established a legal protectorate in Greece in 197/6, nevertheless the conditions of power politics made Greece *de facto* subordinate to Roman foreign policy. So Aymard, pp. 277 ff., and cf. p. 278, n. 16. And cf. also Holleaux, *CAH*, VIII, 196: "Their [*i.e.*, the subject-allies of Philip] freedom was a gift which depended upon Rome's good pleasure."
104. In general see Larsen, *Economic Survey*, IV, 279-80.
105. Larsen, *ibid.*, p. 276.
106. Cf. Livy (A) xxxi. 7. 9.
107. *E.g.*, Livy xxxvi. 12. 2, 8 (by implication), 10.
108. As Walbank maintains, *Philip V*, p. 182; he cites no evidence.
109. In general see Louise E. Matthaei, "On the classification of Roman allies," *CQ*, I (1907), 182-204; Heinrich Horn, *Foederati. Untersuchungen zur Geschichte ihrer Rechtstellung im Zeitalter der römischen Republik und des frühen Principats* (Frankfurt, 1930), esp. p. 11: "Socius ist alles, was nicht civis und nicht hostis ist." The conclusions of Matthaei and Horn were anticipated long ago by Emil Kuhn, *Die städtische und bürgerliche Verfassung des römischen Reichs bis auf die Zeiten Justinians* (2 vols.; Leipzig, 1864-65), II, 21-22. See also P. C. Sands, *The Client Princes of the Roman Empire under the Republic* (Cambridge, 1908), pp. 10 ff.
110. At the beginning of the Third Macedonian War a reference is made to a συμμαχία existing between Epirus and Rome (Polybius xxvii. 15. 12), but a συμμαχία need mean no more than *societas* when applied to Roman matters, cf. Horn, p. 12; Larsen, *CP*, XXX (1935), 202, n. 47; 211.
111. Livy xxxiv. 22. 6.
112. Livy xxxiv. 48. 3.
113. Livy xxxiv. 24. 7; so Oberhummer, p. 177, n. 3. They may have been willing to participate in such a cause for the same reason that they had co-operated with Doson against Cleomenes—fear of social revolution.
114. xxxv. 27. 11: "Inde Tegeam exercitu contracto concilioque eodem et Achaeis et sociis indicto, in quo et Epirotarum et Acarnanum fuere principes . . ."
115. II, 654, n. 1; cf. 683-84 and 684, n. 1. Niese goes farther and cites the passage to prove that the Epirotes and Acarnanians were Roman allies.
116. So Larsen, *CP*, XXX (1935), 202, n. 47; Walbank, *Philip V*, p. 195.
117. See the works cited in the previous note.
118. Aymard, *Premiers rapports*, p. 310, n. 16.
119. There is another matter which is probably germane to the meaning of this passage, but which does little to clarify it. In 192 the city of Thyrrheum in Acarnania and the city of Cassopea in Epirus arbitrated a boundary dispute between the Achaean and Boeotian Leagues, a dispute arising from the transfer of the city of Megara from the latter to the Achaeans. The source is *IG*, VII, 188 and 189, shown by Louis Robert, "Inscriptions de Pagai en Mégaride relatives à un arbitrage," *Revue de philologie, de littérature et d'histoire anciennes*, LXV (1939), 97-122,

at 106 ff., to be parts of one document. Robert thinks that about 192 is the proper date for the readmission of Megara to the Achaean League (so Michel Feyel, *Polybe et l'histoire de Béotie au IIIe siècle avant notre ère* [Paris, 1942], p. 62, n. 1), but on p. 121, n. 3 (cf. p. 115, n. 4) Robert admits that the readmission of Megara, and hence the arbitration, might date from the end of the third century. This earlier date is the one advocated by Aymard, *Premiers rapports*, p. 14, n. 7. If the later date for the affair is correct, however, it might have some bearing on the problem of an alliance between Epirus and Acarnania on the one hand and the Achaeans on the other. Does the arbitration mean that at that time the Epirotes and Acarnanians were not the allies of the Achaeans? For, if they were allies of the latter power, would that fact be sufficient to render them an improper choice for arbitrators from the Boeotian point of view? Unfortunately no clear answer to this question can be made, even supposing that the date 192 is correct. An alliance might have had very limited objectives—the repression of social revolution, for example— and hence been no bar to the disinterested arbitration of the two cities in another matter entirely. The meaning of the passage in Livy is admittedly anything but clear, but the clearest thing about it, it seems, is that Roman *socii* are not meant.

120. Cf. Polybius ix. 37-39, the speech of the Acarnanian Lyciscus; cf. Cato, cited by Pliny *Historia naturalis* xxix. 14.

121. Cf. Polybius xi. 5. 5 ff.

122. See above, pp. 5-6.

123. Cf. Livy xxxiv. 31. 17, where a Greek (Nabis) states in effect that Rome is an oligarchy.

124. Livy xxxiv. 51. 5-6; cf. Larsen, *Economic Survey*, IV, 278-79.

125. Livy xxxiii. 5. 1, xxxv. 34. 3, cf. xxxii. 32. 3.

126. Livy xxxv. 33. 1. cf. xxxii. 32. 1-3.

127. Cf. the discussions in Walbank, *Philip V*, pp. 164-65; Holleaux, *CAH*, VIII, 146.

128. As Alfredo Passerini warns, "Studi di storia ellenistico-romana. VI. I moti politico-sociali della Grecia e i Romani," *Athenaeum*, XI (1933), 309-35.

129. Cf. Holleaux, *CAH*, VIII, 197.

130. For this interpretation of Antiochus' motives, see J. Kromayer, "Hannibal und Antiochos der Grosse, eine politisch-strategische Studie," *Neue Jahrbücher für das klassische Altertum, Geschichte, und deutsche Literatur*, XIX (1907), 681-99, at 684-99; idem, *Schlachtfelder*, II, 130; Maurice Holleaux, "Recherches sur l'histoire des négociations d'Antiochos III avec les Romains," *REA*, XV (1913), 1-24, at 22-23. *Contra:* Passerini, *Athenaeum*, X (1932), 119, n. 7 (on p. 120). For a discussion of the principle of Greek law involved, see Elias Bickermann, "Bellum Antiochicum," *Hermes*, LXVII (1932), 47-76.

131. See above, p. 56.

132. Livy xxxv. 43. 1-6.

133. Livy xxxvi. 1-2; for the "accomplices," see 1. 5-6.

134. Livy xxxv. 23. 5.

135. Livy xxxv. 33. 4, says that Flamininus, addressing the Aetolians, "pauca de iure civitatium de quibus ambigeretur disseruit." He must have mentioned Leucas among such states.

136. Livy xxxv. 23. 4, cf. 25. 5, 37. 3; Holleaux, *CAH*, VIII, 204, n. 2.

137. Livy xxxv. 24. 7, cf. xxxvi. 1. 7; rejecting the two legions given him by

Livy xxxv. 20. 11, 24. 7 (Niese, II, 696, n. 1; Aymard, *Premiers rapports,* p. 327, n. 14; De Sanctis, *Storia,* IV, Part 1, 156, n. 75). From the description of Baebius' operations De Sanctis infers a force of about 2,000 men; Walbank, *Philip V,* p. 199, apparently agrees.
138. Livy xxxvi. 8. 6, 10. 10; Appian *Syriaca* 16; Zonaras ix. 19.3.
139. Livy xxxvi. 11. 2.
140. Livy xxxvi. 11. 8.
141. Livy xxxvi. 5. 1.
142. Polybius xx. 3. 1-4, 6; Livy xxxvi. 5. 1, 3-8.
143. Livy xxxvi. 11. 8. Since Mnasilochus was a member of the embassy sent by Medion to Antiochus (*ibid.* 12.4), he was probably a citizen of that town.
144. Livy xxxvi. 11. 8: "conciliabat" must be conative, since the sequel shows that Acarnania was not won over to Antiochus as a whole.
145. Livy xxxvi. 11. 8-11.
146. Livy xxxvi. 11. 5-7. The account of Polybius must here be considerably compressed by Livy, as was frequently his habit in narrating matters not directly connected with Rome. In the process the passage has become obscure; for example, there is no meaning conveyed by the "ibi" in 11. 8. "Ibi" should refer to Acarnania, but Acarnania has not been mentioned.
147. Livy xxxvi. 12; cf. Appian *Syriaca* 16. We are not told when the garrisons thus placed in Acarnania were removed. The latest possible time is after the battle of Thermopylae, and probably before, since the king would want all his available forces to fight Glabrio; cf. Oberhummer, pp. 179-80 and 180, n. 1. Probably Mnasilochus fled for safety to Antiochus when the troops were withdrawn, for the Romans demanded he be surrendered to them after Magnesia (Polybius xxi. 17. 7, 43. 11; Livy xxxvii. 45. 17, xxxviii. 38. 18). Oberhummer (p. 180) concludes from the flight of Mnasilochus that strong reprisals were taken in Acarnania against the leaders of the anti-Roman party. At the same time that the Romans demanded the surrender of Mnasilochus they also demanded the person of Thoas, the Aetolian, but the latter was returned to the Aetolians at their request (Polybius xxviii. 4. 11-12; Diodorus xxix. 31). It is unlikely that the Acarnanians would ask for Mnasilochus, however, and his fate remains unknown.
148. The later charge, made by a Roman embassy just before the outbreak of the Third Macedonian War, that the Acarnanians had co-operated with Antiochus against Rome much as they had with Philip (Livy xlii. 38. 3), is an exaggeration, designed primarily to throw a scare into the Acarnanians to make them co-operate with the Romans at that time; see below, p. 71.
149. Percy Gardner, "Macedonian and Greek Coins of the Seleucidae," *Numismatic Chronicle and Journal of the Numismatic Society,* n. s., XVIII (1878), 90-102, at 100 ff.; cf. Barclay V. Head, *Historia Numorum* (2nd ed.; Oxford, 1911), pp. 333-34.
150. De Sanctis, *Storia,* IV, Part 1, 157; Walbank, *Philip V,* p. 202.
151. Livy xxxiv. 60. 6.
152. Livy xxxvi. 7. 18-20.
153. Probably the Epirote government was innocent of the exploits of Menestas (or Menestratus, or Menoetas) of Epirus whose importance to the Aetolians was such that Glabrio demanded he be surrendered at the time of his negotiations with the Aetolians in 191 (Polybius xx. 10. 5; Livy xxxvi. 28. 3; cf. Polybius xxi. 31. 13; Livy xxxviii. 10. 6). He was probably a soldier of fortune of Epirote extraction.

154. Livy xxxvi. 35. 8-11; cf. Zonaras ix. 19. 14.
155. Livy xxxvi. 12. 8.
156. Livy xxxvii. 7. 6; cf. Holleaux, *CAH,* VIII, 219.
157. Livy xxxviii. 3. 6, 9.
158. De Sanctis, *Storia,* IV, Part 1, 212.
159. Polybius xxi. 26. 8.
160. Polybius xxi. 26. 1-6; Livy xxxviii. 3. 9 ff. Täubler, p. 218, deduces from Polybius xxi. 26. 1 that the Epirotes concluded a "Feldherrnvertrag" with Nobilior. There is nothing in the passage to warrant such an assumption. Much more likely is merely informal co-operation without definite stipulations.
161. Livy xxxviii. 4. 7, 9.
162. Accepting Niese's conjecture (II, 764, n. 3) of Σιβύρτου τοῦ πειρατοῦ for MSS πετράτου in Polybius xxi. 26. 7.
163. Polybius xxi. 25. 9-11, 26. 7-17.
164. See below, p. 147.
165. Polybius xxi. 29. 1-30. 5; Livy xxxviii. 9.
166. Polybius xxi. 32. 2-14; Livy xxxviii. 11. 2-9.
167. Polybius xxi. 32. 13; Livy xxxviii. 11. 9; cf. Polybius 30. 4; Livy 9. 10. There are discrepancies in the date *post quem,* but the matter does not affect Ambracia, for by any possible interpretation of the various accounts that city was lost to the Aetolians.
168. Livy xxxviii. 44. 4-5; cf. *SEG,* III, 451, with the discussion of Maurice Holleaux, "Fragment de Sénatus-conulte trouvé à Corfou," *BCH,* XLVIII (1924), 381-98. The provision about *portoria* seems without precedent (cf. Frank, *AHR,* XVIII (1912-13), 236. Perhaps the provision was intended to favor possible Latin (and Roman?) residents (*negotiatores*) of Ambracia. If so, it might have been in recompense for services rendered in connection with the siege of the city. There were Italians residing in Greece at this time; cf. Livy xxxiii. 17. 11, 28. 3; Hatzfeld, pp. 22-23, dating *SGDI,* 1339 (Epirote) and *IG,* IX, 1, 513 (Acarnanian) proxeny decrees to this period.
169. Livy xxxviii. 4. 10, 5. 6.
170. Polybius xxi. 29. 4; Livy xxxviii. 9. 2, 5.
171. See above, p. 34.
172. Polybius xxi. 32. 14; Livy xxxviii. 11. 9; Dionysius Halicarnassensis i. 51. 2. Dionysius is the sole authority (in a very confused passage) for the Echinades, and his expression is vague; the Acarnanians are to "enjoy" (καρποῦσθαι) the islands in common with the Aetolians. In view of the silence of Polybius, who is probably giving either the treaty itself or a detailed summary of it, and the confusion prevailing in this passage of Dionysius (see below, appendix, pp. 92-97), the clause about the islands should probably be rejected. Oberhummer, p. 186, n. 1, accepts the passage and interprets it to mean a division of the islands between Aetolia and Acarnania. This is possible, of course—but if so, why did Dionysius use the peculiar word "enjoy"? It might mean enjoy the produce, or the revenues, but in any case is very vague.
173. Propaganda incorporated as history by Justin (Trogus) xxviii. 1. 5-2. 14. See below, appendix, pp. 92-97.
174. See above, p. 34.
175. See Aemilius Sura, cited in Velleius Paterculus i. 6. 6 (an interpolated pas-

sage) and cf. J. W. Swain, "The Theory of the Four Monarchies. Opposition History Under the Roman Empire," *CP*, XXXV (1940), 1-21, at 2-3 and 3, n. 5, who shows that the passage is to be dated to 189-71. The theory of the four monarchies is Asiatic (Swain, pp. 4-5), but it evidently found some acceptance at Rome in this period.

Chapter IV

1. See the list of embassies in Larsen, *Economic Survey*, IV, 286-90. At least one item could be added to this list; cf. *SEG*, III, 451, with the commentary of Maurice Holleaux, *BCH*, XLVIII (1924), 381-98. Our literary sources probably restrict themselves to those of the most important general interest.
2. Polybius xxiii. 1. 10-12; cf. Livy xxxix. 46. 6-9. Livy does not mention the Epirotes. Pausanias vii. 8. 6 mentions Epirote complaints in 185 (cf. 9. 1), but Polybius and Livy make no mention of Epirote affairs in connection with that year. Hence Pausanias has probably confused two separate matters, or by "Epirote" means "Athamanians"; cf. Polybius xxii. 6. 3; Livy xxxix. 24. 8. The Athamanians were frequently considered an Epirote people (see above, Ch. I, n. 48).
3. Polybius xxiii. 4. 16; Livy xxxix. 48. 5. For the chronology, see André Aymard, "Les stratèges de la confédération achéene de 202 à 172 av. J.-C.," *REA*, XXX (1928), 1-62, at 27-28.
4. Polybius xxiii. 8. 2; cf. Livy xxxix. 53. 10.
5. Cf. Walbank, *Philip V*, pp. 226 ff., esp. 232.
6. Polybius xxiv. 8. 9-9. 15, 10. 7. On the date, 180 B.C., see Aymard, *REA*, XXX (1928), 58-61.
7. Polybius xxiv. 10. 6.
8. Cf. Walbank, *Philip V*, pp. 223-57, esp. 256-57.
9. An interesting list of them is found in a Delphic inscription (*SIG*³, 643).
10. Polybius xxv. 3. 1-3. For Perseus and social unrest generally, see Fritz Geyer, *s.v.* "Perseus" (5), *RE*, XIX (1937-38), cols. 996-1021, at 1002-3.
11. Livy xlii. 12. 7, 40. 7; Diodorus Siculus xxix. 36 (33); cf. Polybius xxx. 11.
12. Polybius xxv. 3. 4, xxvii. 9. 1, 10. 1; cf. Livy xlii. 63. 2; Appian *Macedonica* 11.1.
13. Polybius xxx. 12 (cf. xxx. 11). This is a description of affairs in 167, but such social and economic disorders do not arise suddenly.
14. Livy xlii. 37. 1 ff. For the interpretation of the embassy and the chronology, see F. W. Walbank, "A Note on the Embassy of Q. Marcius Philippus, 172 B.C.," *JRS*, XXXI (1941), 82-93. (Cf. Livy xlii. 52. 8.) For an analysis of the difficulties involved in reconstructing a coherent account from Livy, who dates the embassy a year late, and for the general chronology of the outbreak of the Third Macedonian War, see De Sanctis, *Storia*, IV, Part 1, 398-400.
15. Livy xlii. 37. 4.
16. It was probably situated near Phanote (cf. Polybius xxvii. 16. 5); so Niese, III, 112, n. 4.
17. Livy xlii. 38. 1; cf. Appian *Macedonica* 11. 4.
18. Appian *Macedonica* 11. 4, lists Acarnania among the places visited. He is

probably wrong, or has confused the Acarnanian embassy to the Romans with a Roman visit to Acarnania itself.
19. Livy xlii. 38. 3-4.
20. Livy xlii. 43. 1-2.
21. Livy xlii. 36. 1-7 = 48. 1-3.
22. Livy xlii. 30. 8-11.
23. Livy xlii. 32. 4.
24. Livy xlii. 18. 2-3. For the month see Walbank, *JRS*, XXXI (1941), 82 and n. 4. The passage of Livy is Polybian according to Nissen, p. 246; but annalistic according to Walbank, *ibid.*, p. 85. Cf. also Livy xlii. 27. 6, 36.8.
25. Livy xlii. 47. 11.
26. Livy xlii. 49. 10, 55. 1-2.
27. De Sanctis, *Storia*, IV, Part 1, 286-87.
28. Livy xlii. 55. 2.
29. Livy xlii. 67. 9.
30. See above, pp. 1, 47-48.
31. For what follows concerning the parties in Epirus in 170 and the years immediately preceding the source is Polybius xxvii. 15 (cf. Diodorus Siculus xxx. 5) unless otherwise specified.
32. Polybius xxx. 13. 4.
33. See below, p. 76.
34. xxvii. 15. 7-8.
35. Cf. Polybius xxx. 7. 1-4.
36. He alone is mentioned by Polybius xxvii. 15. 10 ff.; cf. Livy, xliii. 18. 2.
37. Polybius xxvii. 15. 12.
38. xlii. 38. 1.
39. Polybius xxx. 7. 1. Cephalus is probably to be identified with the Cephalus who was *prostates* of the Molossian tribe in this period (*SGDI*, 1352 = Constantin Carapanos, *Dodone et ses ruines* [2 vols.; Paris, 1878], II, Pl. XXX, no. 2; cf. I, 57-58, no. 11).
40. Polybius xxvii. 15. 10.
41. Polybius xxx. 7. 3-4.
42. For Pyrrhus as a Molossian see the inscriptions recorded in Plutarch *Pyrrhus* 26; for the end of Molossian predominance with the fall of the monarchy, Cross, p. 97; H. H. Scullard, "Charops and Roman Policy in Epirus," *JRS*, XXXV (1945), 58-64, at 58.
43. The poverty of Molossis is possibly shown by the fact that the thorough plundering of the country in 167 allotted only eleven drachmas apiece to the soldiers of Aemilius Paulus according to Plutarch (*Aemilius Paulus* 29). Livy (xlv. 34. 5) gives much higher figures, which are to be accepted, as De Sanctis (*Storia*, IV, Part 1, 350, n. 300 on 351) shows. But Livy (*ibid.*, 6) is plainly giving the total booty, including the 150,000 slaves. Plutarch's figures are so very different that it is possible he is proceeding on a different basis of calculation; that his figure represents the value received from the sale of the inanimate property only. It was to the interest of the moralist to show so small a gain from so large a destruction. De Sanctis' defense of Livy's figures rests primarily on the reckoning in of the price of the slaves. That the places pillaged were mainly in Molossis is borne out by Polybius, cited by Strabo vii. 322. M. Cary, *The Geographic Background of Greek and Roman History* (Oxford,

1949), p. 58, speaks of the fertility of Molossis and seems to conclude that the economic strength of Molossis was a principal reason for its dominating position in Epirote politics in the fourth and third centuries. This may well be so; but if so, one might also argue in the opposite direction that the decline of Molossian influence in Epirus from the end of the third century may well have been a symptom of decline in relative economic strength.

44. The sources for the attempted kidnapping of Mancinus are Polybius xxvii. 16; Diodorus Siculus xxx. 5a = Müller, *Excerpta* Diodori Siculi, *FHG*, II, p. ix, fr. 7.
45. Polybius xxvii. 16. 4, calls him κρωπίῳ, which seems to be meaningless. Possibly the text should be emended to Ὠρωπίῳ, for there seems to have been an Oropus in Epirus; see Schweighäuser *ad Polybium* xxvii. 14. 4 (= 16. 4, Büttner-Wobst).
46. Polybius xxvii. 16.5, says that he divined the plot in some supernatural manner.
47. Polybius xxvii. 16. 3, speaks of the Molossians without qualification.
48. Polybius xxvii. 15. 14-16.
49. Livy xlii. 59. 1; cf. Polybius xxvii. 9. 1; Livy xlii. 63. 1.
50. Polybius xxvii. 15. 15-16.
51. Livy xliii. 18. 2.
52. xxx. 5a = Müller, *Excerpta* Diodori Siculi, *FHG*, II, p. ix, fr. 7.
53. Polybius xxvii. 16. 1.
54. Livy xliii. 18. 1-2; cf. Polybius xxx. 7. 2-4.
55. Livy xliii. 21. 5.
56. Polybius xxx. 15 (= Strabo vii. 322) implies that not all the places punished in 167 were in Molossis. Zonaras ix. 22. 7, exaggerates when he says "most of Epirus."
57. Livy xliii. 21. 4, xlv. 26. 3.
58. So De Sanctis, *Storia*, IV, Part 1, 294; and see below, p. 82.
59. Probably most of Chaonia and Thesprotis remained loyal to Rome; cf. Livy xliii. 21. 4.
60. Cf. Kromayer, *Schlachtfelder*, II, 261; Scullard, *JRS*, XXXV (1945), 58; Larsen, *Economic Survey*, IV, 290.
61. Livy puts the embassy in 169, but it probably belongs to 170 because immediately after the conclusion of the embassy's travels Popilius, one of the envoys, was sent into winter quarters by Mancinus (Livy xliii. 17. 10).
62. Polybius xxviii. 3. 1, 4. 13, 5. 1-6; cf. Livy xliii. 17. 2-10.
63. Polybius xxviii. 5. 6.
64. Livy xliii. 17. 10.
65. Cf. Niese, III, 138.
66. Livy xliii. 18. 1.
67. His status is uncertain; he was not the commander of the Roman forces in Illyria. Livy (A) xliii. 9. 6 ff. is to be corrected by Livy (P) xliii. 21. 1.
68. Livy xliii. 21. 4. Possibly Athamanians instead of Chaonians are meant. The text is corrupt; the MS reads "THOANUM." In defense of Chaonians instead of Athamanians, see J. N. Madvig, *Emendationes Livianae* (2nd ed.; Copenhagen, 1877), pp. 673-74.
69. Livy xliii. 21. 4-5.

70. Livy xliii. 21. 5.
71. Livy xliii. 21. 6, wrongly locates the city geographically. His principal source here is Polybius, but this remark about the importance and location of Stratus is probably an "explanation" added by Livy himself for the benefit of his Roman readers.
    Possibly a Molossian force under Philostratus accompanied Perseus. There were Epirotes with him (Livy xliii. 22. 9) and some time elapses before the Molossians under Philostratus join Clevas in his pursuit of Appius Claudius (*ibid.*, 23. 3). If the force under Philostratus simply arrived too late to help Clevas in raising the siege, too long a time would probably elapse merely to account for Molossian mobilization and march to Phanote.
72. Livy xliii. 21. 5ff.
73. Livy xliii. 22. 9-10.
74. Larsen, *Economic Survey*, IV, 290.
75. Livy xliii. 23. 1-6.
76. Kromayer, *Schlachtfelder*, p. 265 and n. 1. Even if Claudius were unable to do more than take Phanote, at which of course he failed, he would have begun the process of reducing the revolted Epirotes. That Phanote was the proper place to begin is shown by the fact that Anicius began his Epirote campaign in 168 by a march to Phanote, which surrendered. It is also probably not without significance that Phanote dominates the land route from Corcyra (the Roman naval base) to Illyria. It was probably by this route that Flamininus traveled to the Roman camp in the Aous valley in 198 (see above, p. 46).
77. Livy xliv. 1. 1-4.
78. Livy xliv. 1. 3-4.
79. Polybius xxviii. 13. 7 ff.
80. *Ibid.*, 11. Fortunately we need not enter here into a discussion of why Marcius did not want Claudius to have the soldiers. Polybius' whole account strikes one as rather disingenuous. For various explanations, see W. E. Heitland, *The Roman Republic* (3 vols.; Cambridge [England], 1909), II, 104; Tenney Frank, "The Diplomacy of Q. Marcius in 169 B.C.," *CP*, V (1910), 358-61; De Sanctis, *Storia*, IV, Part 1, 307; P. V. M. Benecke, "The Fall of the Macedonian Monarchy," *CAH*, VIII (Cambridge [England], 1930), 241-78, at 266.
81. Livy xliv. 16. 2.
82. For the date see De Sanctis, *Storia*, IV, Part 1, 369-76 on Livy xliv. 37. 8. Benjamin D. Meritt has published an inscription which places the June dating beyond doubt; see "The Inscriptions," "The American Excavations in the Athenian Agora, Third Report," *Hesperia*, III (1934), 1-128, at 18-21 (no. 18); and for a more recent edition, also by Meritt, "Greek Inscriptions," "The American Excavations in the Athenian Agora, Tenth Report," *ibid.*, V (1936), 355-441, at 429-30 (no. 17). On the relationship of this date in the Julian calendar to the Roman (Flavian) calendar of the time, see S. I. Oost, "The Roman Calendar in the Year of Pydna (168 B.C.)," *CP*, XLVIII (1953), 217-30.
83. Livy xlv. 26. 3-11; cf. Polybius xxx. 7. 2-4. Livy puts these events under 167, erroneously. The winter of 167-66 cannot be meant, for Anicius triumphed at Rome in 167 (cf. Livy xlv. 43. 1 and the *Fasti Triumphales*).
84. Polybius xxx. 13. 1-6; Livy xlv. 31. 6 ff.
85. Polybius xxx. 13. 6-7; Livy xlv. 31. 9.
86. At least in the case of Achaea, and probably in the other cases also, if the judgment of Polybius be accepted (xxx. 13. 11).

87. Polybius vii. 9. 14.
88. Livy xlv. 18.
89. Livy xlv. 30. 6.
90. See above, p. 52.
91. Fine, *TAPA*, LXIII (1932), 129-30.
92. *Ibid.;* see also above, p. 77.
93. Fine, *TAPA*, LXIII (1932), 128; cf. Strabo vii. fr. 47 (48) (Jones), who says that Paulus added some Epirote tribes to Macedonia IV. The name "Tymphaea" is an emendation; the MS reads: "AUTINCANIA ESTRYMEPALISETELIMO/NITES." Geography, however, shows that the emendation to "Tymphaea" is correct. Otherwise Atintania would be completely isolated from the rest of Macedonia IV. There would be no connection through Illyria, for Philip had had to give up his gains of 205 in Illyria after the Second Macedonian War.
94. Livy xlv. 31. 12.
95. As the coinage seems to indicate; cf. Head, p. 330.
96. Livy xlv. 26. 11. cf. 17. 1, 4.
97. Livy xlv. 26. 15.
98. Livy xlv. 26. 12-15.
99. Livy xlv. 26. 3-10.
100. Heuss, p. 63. On *deditio* see also above, p. 13.
101. Livy xlv. 33. 8. The statement in Appian *Illyrica* 9 is an obvious confusion with what happened in Epirus.
102. The sources are Polybius xxx. 15 (= Strabo vii. 322); Livy xlv. 34. 1-9; Plutarch *Aemilius Paulus* 29; Trogus Pompeius *Prologi* 33; Eutropius iv. 8; Appian *Illyrica* 9 (related of Illyria by mistake); Pliny *Historia naturalis* iv. 39 (related of Macedonia by mistake). For the "freedom" of the Epirotes, see J. A. O. Larsen, "*Consilium* in Livy xlv. 18. 6-7 and the Macedonian *synedria*," *CP*, XLIV (1949), 73-90, at 84; *idem*, *Economic Survey*, IV, 302. Niese's belief (III, 187) that Molossis and the other places that had been punished were separated from the *koinon* is based on no evidence and seems unlikely. Rome had no reason to wish tc be responsible for an exhausted country with but a handful of inhabitants left.
103. Livy xlv. 34. 8-9.
104. Polybius xxxii. 5. 6. The text is difficult, but this seems to be the sense. I am not convinced, however, of the wisdom of adding the name of Aemilius Paulus here. The text does not necessarily require any addition as it stands, if *kai* be bracketed as Hultsch wishes.
105. Polybius xxx. 13. 6; Livy xlv. 31. 9.
106. Livy xlv. 34. 1; cf. Plutarch *Aemilius Paulus* 29. Plutarch, *ibid.*, 30, says that what he did was repugnant to Paulus' mild nature. But it must be remembered that this statement is probably to be traced to Polybius, the boon companion of Scipio Aemilianus, Paulus' son. Polybius has also said (xxx. 13. 11) that Paulus personally objected to the vendetta against the anti-Roman and neutral leaders in Achaea. Scullard, *JRS*, XXXV (1945), 59-60, nevertheless accepts the judgment of Polybius because: (1) Paulus was a stern disciplinarian and hence would not want his troops to pillage Epirus because of the slackening of discipline involved. (2) Paulus detested the Epirote Charops whom Scullard accuses of being the person primarily responsible for the outrage in Molossis. (3) Paulus' troops were dissatisfied with the booty they received, especially

since they had not been permitted to plunder Macedonia (Livy xlv. 35-39). On the other hand: (1) Paulus might have been willing to throw his troops a plum, after refusing to let them plunder Macedonia, and that too probably in conformity with the wishes of the senate. As far as discipline was concerned, the pillaging of Epirus was a thoroughly well-organized and controlled undertaking, as I have tried to show in the text. (2) It is not proved that Charops was responsible for the pillaging of Epirus (see below, n. 112), and if he wasn't, he was a sufficiently unprincipled person (cf. Polybius xxxii. 5-6) for Paulus to detest him (*ibid.*, 6. 5). Indeed, Polybius strongly implies ($\pi\nu\theta\alpha\nu\acute{o}\mu\epsilon\nu\text{o}\iota$) that Paulus learned about Charops' crimes on the occasion of the latter's visit to Rome. The crimes concerned then must be those committed since 167. These were the crimes which made Paulus refuse to see Charops. (3) The last point is not relevant. The troops were dissatisfied with the amount of booty. Paulus could not supply it where it wasn't to be had. And as far as pillaging Molossis was concerned, he had obviously done as thorough a job as possible. Accordingly, the question whether Paulus approved of the punishment of Epirus or not is an open one.

107. Benecke, *CAH*, VIII (1930), 272.
108. As Scullard, *JRS*, XXXV (1945), 60, points out.
109. *Ibid.*, 58-64; cf. *idem, Politics*, p. 213.
110. xxx. 12. 2-3.
111. Polybius xxvii. 15. 5.
112. It may be well to consider Scullard's argument in greater detail. If Charops actually was the person primarily responsible for the destruction of seventy communities and the enslavement of 150,000 persons, he almost certainly was the most ferocious and unprincipled contemporary of Polybius, or of any past age that Polybius knew. But could he not still be the most ferocious and unprincipled man Polybius knew of without descending to this particular depth of infamy? Scullard himself (pp. 61-62) speaks of merely hazarding a guess about the nature of his crime. And allowance must also be made for the possibility that Polybius' indignation may have carried him away and led him into making a stronger statement, for rhetorical reasons, than may actually have been true. Scullard asks if Charops was worse for ordinary crimes than Callicrates, who was the chief pro-Roman lickspittle in Achaea, Polybius' own country. Polybius would thus feel the crimes of Callicrates more immediately than those of Charops. The crimes of Charops must have been enormous indeed to have bested this record in Polybius' mind. It is quite possible that the ordinary crimes of Charops in Epirus were greater than those of Callicrates in Achaea. Charops is said to have committed every sort of crime in Epirus, to have murdered and assassinated people there as he pleased, and to have confiscated the goods of those he slew (Polybius xxxii. 5). In other words, he seemed to unite the vices of a Callicrates with those of a Nabis (aside from the social question). Callicrates seems never to have gone so far as this. Had he even been in a position to do so, the citizens would not have refused to bathe after him (Polybius xxx. 29. 2 ff.)—out of fear.

There is a good probability that the family of Charops was Chaonian, or at least from northwestern Epirus, as Scullard shows (p. 62). The elder Charops in 198 would much more easily have contacted a shepherd who knew the way around the Aous gorges, if he were a *princeps* of Chaonia or some place near by, than if his family were situated elsewhere. But even if Charops was a Chaonian, and even if thereby he was the hereditary enemy of the Molossians, that proves nothing. Undoubtedly the action of Rome in Epirus is to be traced to the unprincipled men who were coming to power in the period of the Third Macedonian War (Scullard, pp. 62-63). Yet it is quite possible that men who, in other situations, had acted completely without regard for international usage or common humanity in treating the Greeks and other peoples (see the list in Scullard, *ibid.*) required no suggestion from Charops to ravage Molossis systematically; as they required no suggestion to maltreat Carthage before and after the Third Punic War.

It is probably correct to infer that Paulus had received instructions about Molossis and the "revolted" Epirotes after the dispatch to the east of the commissions for Macedonia and Illyria (autumn, 168), inasmuch as Anicius had to be warned ahead of time of what Paulus was about to do (Livy xlv. 34. 1; cf. Scullard, p. 60); but the gang in the senate could issue supplementary instructions of this sort without outside stimulation. (On Paulus' personal aversion to Charops and its meaning, see above, n. 106.)

Hence Scullard's theory is interesting and attractive, but there is no direct proof of it, and the circumstantial evidence is not strong enough. *Non liquet.*

113. These and other instances are pointed out by Scullard, *JRS*, XXXV (1945), 62-63.
114. Cf. Polybius i. 1. 5, 3. 1, 5. 1, iii. 1. 9; Larsen, *CP*, XXX (1935), 206-7.
115. See Vincenzo Costanzi, "La condizione giuridica della Grecia dopo la distruzione di Corinto nel 146 a. Chr.," *Rivista di filologia*, XLV (1917), 402-23.
116. With the probable exception of the payment of tribute.
117. SIG^3, 653A, 4; 653B, 22? (= *Fouilles de Delphes*, III, 1, 218j); 654A, 4 (= *Fouilles de Delphes*, III, 2, 135, 4).
118. Polybius xxx. 12. 1, cf. xxx. 11.
119. Head, p. 325.
120. xxx. 12. 2-3.
121. Polybius xxxii. 5. 5-6. 2; Diodorus Siculus xxxi. 42 (31).
122. The *terminus ante quem* is the death of Aemilius Paulus which occurred in this year (Didascalicum in Terentii *Adelphous;* Livy *Ep.* xlvi).
123. Polybius xxxii. 6. 3.
124. For what Charops hoped to do, see the similar procedure described in SIG^3, 656, ll. 20 ff.
125. Polybius xxxii. 6. 3-9.
126. Polybius xxxii. 5. 4.
127. Cf. Scullard, *JRS*, XXXV (1945), 61. Th. Büttner-Wobst, *s.v.*, "Charops" (12), *RE*, Supp. I (1903), col. 285, thinks that Charops died almost at once after his embassy to Rome (*ca.* 160 B.C.), but perhaps this does not allow enough time for Charops to get home, for the embassy to follow him to Epirus and return, and for Charops to go to Italy again.
128. Polybius xxxii. 14.
129. Polybius xxx. 32. 8-12.
130. Polybius iii. 5. 4.
131. Polybius xxxv. 6 (= Plutarch *Cato Major* 9); Pausanias vii. 10. 12.
132. SIG^3, 669; cf. *IG*, IX, 1, 513-7. In 94 B.C. Thyrrheum was given a treaty with Rome (SIG^3, 732). What this means for the Acarnanian *koinon* is doubtful; cf. Oberhummer, pp. 197-98.
133. For Thyrrheum as capital of Acarnania after 167, see Busolt-Swoboda II, 1468 and n. 4.

134. Head, p. 329.
135. *IG.* IX, 1, 516, l. 7. For the date see the commentaries on 513-15 and on *SIG*³, 669.
136. Polybius xxxii. 5. 2, cf. xxx. 13. 4.
137. See Larsen, *Economic Survey*, IV, 303 and references cited there.
138. Rostovtzeff, II, 763.

Appendix

1. xxviii. 1-2.
2. *Rome*, pp. 5-22.
3. Polybius ii. 12. 7.
4. *Rome*, pp. 16-19.
5. Polybius ix. 32. 3-39. 7.
6. Thus pretty well disposing of W. W. Tarn's view (*Antigonos Gonatas*, p. 383, n. 38) that Justin's narrative is so circumstantial that "it is hard to believe that it has no foundation."
7. *Hermes*, LXVIII (1933), 144.
8. "Die Kriegsschuldfrage von 218 v. Chr. Geb.," *Sitzungsberichte der Heidelberger Akademie der Wissenschaften*, Philosophisch-historische Klasse, XXIV (1934), 4. Abh., 26 and n. 1.
9. Eduard Meyer, *Kleine Schriften*, II, 382, n. 1, accepts the fact of the appeal and the Roman response. His essay was published in 1924 (see p. 332), three years after Holleaux's book, but he gives no evidence of acquaintance with Holleaux's work here. Fritz Geyer, *s.v.* "Makedonien (Geschichte)," *RE*, XIV (1930), cols. 697-771, at 743-4 also accepts the embassy without further ado. Beloch, IV, Part 1, 634, 664, accepts the Acarnanian appeal and the Roman embassy. He expressly rejects Holleaux (634, n. 3), remarking that "Polybius kann seine Gründe gehabt haben, den diplomatischen Misserfolg der Römer zu verschweigen"; thus he minimizes Polybius' statement (ii. 17. 2) about the first Roman embassies to Greece; but Beloch does not explain further.
10. xxviii. 1. 6.
11. x. 462.
12. i. 51. 2.
13. Θούριος usually means a man from Thurii, but Stephanus Byzantinus (*s.v.* Θυρέα) cites Androtion as using it of Thyrium (or Thyreum, or Thyrrheum), the Acarnanian city. From what follows Dionysius obviously is using it in the latter sense. On Patron, cf. Vergil *Aeneid* v. 298.
14. xxi. 32. 14; cf. Livy xxxviii. 11. 9.
15. *Rome*, p. 19, n. 1 (on p. 20). Holleaux shows that the anti-Roman arrogance of the Justin passage matches well the insolence shown by the Aetolians toward the Romans in 192-89 B.C., citing Livy xxxv. 33, 9-11 (cf. xxxvi. 24. 12), xxxv. 48. 11-13, xxxvii. 49. 1-2. This is the well-known Aetolian *intemperantia linguae* (Livy xxxv. 48, 11). "Il semble que la légende ait pris naissance après la guerre syro-aitolique, sous la vive impression que cette guerre avait laissé dans les esprits." Why not during the war, when Aetolian pride and *intemperantia* would naturally be highest?

16. *Rome*, p. 13, n. 4, following Niese, II, 264, n. 6.
17. *Rome*, p. 19, n. 1, and p. 13. n. 4.
18. See above, pp. 53-54.
19. *Rome*, pp. 13-14 and 13, n. 4.
20. x. 460.
21. This meaning of "autonomy" bars relating this grant of "autonomy" to the grant of the right to "use their own laws" of the *senatusconsultum* of winter 197/6 (Polybius xviii. 44. 2). Moreover, whatever the senate meant by that grant of 197/6, that grant was of a general nature. Strabo seems to imply a particular act relating to the Acarnanians specifically; of course Justin says so explicitly.
22. Livy xlv. 17-18.
23. On *libertas* as the condition of not being subject to another people, see Proculus *Digest* xlix. 15. 7. 1: "Liber...populus est is qui nullius alterius potestati est subiectus...."
24. See Jacoby, *Fr. Gr. H.*, IIC, 220 ff.
25. Strabo iv. 188, xv. 711. Note also that the mythological grounds for the favor in Strabo and Justin are the same, but different in Dionysius. It is thought that Dionysius did not make use of Timagenes (Jacoby, IIC, 222, 224).
26. Or Acarnanian requests for all the "lost cities"; see below, p. 96.
27. It may be objected that Dionysius relates the Trojan War argument to the favors conferred by Rome both in 197/6 and in 189. It would be quite easy for a careless historian, relating favors granted by the Romans to the Acarnanians, to make one explanation do for all of them. One may also notice that this passage contains at least one egregious error—the statement that the Romans took Leucas and Anactorium from the Corinthians. As far as Dionysius' true information goes, the information about the Aetolians, Dionysius dates the Roman favor to 189.
28. See above, pp. 54-55.
29. *SIG*[3], 591, ll. 20 ff. Possibly the people of Lampsacus did not succeed in their object (see Elias Bickermann, "Rom und Lampsakos," *Philogus*, LXXXVII [1932], 299-99, at 291-99), but this does not affect the grounds on which they made the attempt. The appeal to mythology both by Lampsacus and by Acarnania is, of course, but formal. Flamininus himself evidently accepted the Aeneas story and proclaimed it in the inscriptions on his offerings at Delphi (Plutarch *Flamininus* 12). Such inscriptions on such gifts at a principal center of Greece would command wide attention. Plutarch obviously refers these offerings to the period 196-94 of Flamininus' settlement of Greece after the Second Macedonian War. Further than that, to argue from the order of Plutarch's narrative that the offerings follow the Isthmian proclamation (*ibid.*, 10) and precede the war with Nabis (*ibid.*, 13) would be unsafe. If such argumentation were permitted, however, note that this publication of the Aeneas story follows the settlement of Acarnanian affairs (see above, p. 54), but this in turn also means little. The Acarnanians might or might not have previously been aware of the Romans' readiness to accept the story of their Trojan origin.
30. See above, p. 54.
31. xxviii. 2. 14.
32. See above, p. 65.
33. *Rome*, p. 19, n. 1.
34. "Ab omni genere [or onere] immunes," Suetonius *Claudius* 25. David Magie, *Roman Rule in Asia Minor* (2 vols.; Princeton, 1950), II,

943-44, maintains with reason that the "tradition of the letter of Seleucus" is a Greek (Ilian) rather than a Roman fabrication.
35. Jacoby, No. 88, esp. T 8; cf. Plutarch *Moralia* 68B; see Jacoby's commentary on T 8 (IIC, p. 223); on Timagenes and anti-Roman propaganda see also E. M. Sanford, "Contrasting Views of the Roman Empire," *AJP,* LVIII (1937), 437-56, at 440-41.
36. See above, n. 15.
37. Meyer, *Kleine Schriften,* II, 382, n. 1, regards the Aetolian speceh as "a free composition of Trogus himself." Trogus (or Timagenes, or whatever was Trogus' source) may have given the "speech" its present form, but that does not exclude the possibility that the author of the speech had a tale of Aetolian defiance of the Romans to go on. The whole speech so well fits the sort of thing the Aetolians are known to have been saying in 192-189. Martin Schanz, *Geschichte der römischen Literatur bis zum Gesetzgebungswerk des Kaisers Justinian,* II (4th ed.; Munich, 1935), ed by Carl Hosius, 322, points out the note of jarring hostility to Rome in the speech, and implies that the hostility is owing to Trogus' Greek source. It seems unlikely that Trogus himself was as hostile to Rome as he has usually been thought to be, inasmuch as he was proud to relate the achievements of his grandfather, father, and uncle in her service (Justin xliii. 5. 11-12). Trogus' hostility to Rome is rejected by Alfred Klotz, s.v. "Pompeius" No. 142, *RE,* XXI, Part 2 Stuttgart, 1952), 2300-2313, at 2308.

ROMAN HISTORY

An Arno Press Collection

Accame, Silvio. **Il Dominio Romano in Grecia Dalla Guerra Acaica Ad Augusto.** 1946

Berchem, Denis van. **Les Distributions De Blé Et D'Argent À La Plèbe Romaine Sous L'Empire.** 1939

Bouché-Leclercq, A[uguste]. **Histoire De La Divination Dans L'Antiquité.** Four Volumes in Two. 1879/1880/1882

Cagnat, René [Louis Victor]. **L'Armée Romaine D'Afrique Et L'Occupation Militaire De L'Afrique Sous Les Empereurs.** Two Parts in One. 1913

Chilver, G[uy] E[dward] F[arquhar]. **Cisalpine Gaul:** Social and Economic History From 49 B.C. To The Death of Trajan. 1941

Crook, John [A]. **Consilium Principis;** Imperial Councils and Counsellors From Augustus To Diocletian. 1955

Cuntz, Otto. **Die Geographie Des Ptolemaeus:** Galliae, Germania, Raetia, Noricum, Pannoniae, Illyricum, Italia. 1923

Déléage, André. **La Capitation Du Bas-Empire.** 1945

Delehaye, Hippolyte. **Les Légendes Grecques Des Saints Militaires.** 1909

Dessau, Hermann. **Geschichte Der Römischen Kaiserzeit.** Three Parts in Two. 1924/1926/1930

Doer, Bruno. **Die Römische Namengebung:** Ein Historischer Versuch. 1937

Fritz, Kurt von. **The Theory of the Mixed Constitution in Antiquity;** A Critical Analysis of Polybius' Political Ideas. 1954

[Fronto, Marcus Cornelius]. **M. Cornelii Frontonis Epistulae, Adnotatione Critica Instructae.** Edited by Michael Petrus Iosephus van den Hout. 1954

Grosse, Robert. **Römische Militärgeschichte Von Gallienus Bis Zum Beginn Der Byzantinischen Themenverfassung.** 1920

Hardy, E[rnest] G[eorge]. **Roman Laws and Charters** And **Three Spanish Charters and Other Documents.** Translated With Introductions and Notes. 1912/1912

Hasebroek, Johannes. **Untersuchungen Zur Geschichte Des Kaisers Septimius Severus.** 1921

Hatzfeld, Jean. **Les Trafiquants Italiens Dans L'Orient Hellénique.** 1919

Hirschfeld, Otto. **Kleine Schriften.** 1913

Holleaux, Maurice. ΣΤΡΑΤΗΓΟΣ ΤΠΑΤΟΣ: Étude Sur La Traduction En Grec Du Titre Consulaire. 1918

Hüttl, Willy. **Antoninus Pius.** Two Volumes in One. 1936/1933

Laet, Siegfried J. De. **Portorium**: Étude Sur L'Organisation Douanière Chez Les Romains, Surtout À L'Epoque Du Haut-Empire. 1949

Magie, David. **Roman Rule in Asia Minor to the End of the Third Century After Christ.** Two Volumes. 1950

Marquardt, Joachim. **Römische Staatsverwaltung.** Three Volumes. 1881/1884/1885

Meltzer, Otto and Ulrich Kahrstedt. **Geschichte Der Karthager.** Three Volumes. 1879/1896/1913

[Nicephorus (Patriarch of Constantinople). Edited by Carl Gotthard de Boor]. **Nicephori Archiepiscopi Constantinopolitani Opuscula Historica.** Edited by Carolus de Boor. 1880

Nissen, Heinrich. **Kritische Untersuchungen Über Die Quellen Der Vierten Und Fünften Dekade Des Livius.** 1863

Oost, Stewart Irvin. **Roman Policy in Epirus and Acarnania in the Age of the Roman Conquest of Greece.** 1954

Paribeni, Roberto. **Optimus Princeps**: Saggio Sulla Storia E Sui Tempi Dell' Imperatore Traiano. Two Volumes in One. 1926/1927

Ramsay, W[illiam] M[itchell]. **The Cities and Bishoprics of Phrygia**: Being An Essay of the Local History of Phrygia From the Earliest Times to the Turkish Conquest. Two Parts in One. 1895/1897

Rosenberg, Arthur. **Untersuchungen Zur Römischen Zenturienverfassung.** 1911

Sands, P[ercy] C[ooper]. **The Client Princes of the Roman Empire Under the Republic.** 1908

Schulten, Adolf. **Geschichte Von Numantia.** 1933

Schulten, Adolf. **Sertorius.** 1926

Scriptores Originum Constantinopolitanarum. Edited by Theodorus Preger. Two Parts in One. 1901/1907

Smith, R[ichard] E[dwin]. **The Failure of the Roman Republic.** 1955

Studies in Cassius Dio and Herodian: H. A. Andersen and E. Hohl. 1975

Studies in the Social War: A. Kiene, E. Marcks, I. Haug and A. Voirol. 1975

Sundwall, Johannes. **Abhandlungen zur Geschichte Des Ausgehenden Römertums.** 1919

Sydenham, Edward A[llen]. **The Coinage of the Roman Republic.** Revised with Indexes by G. C. Haines, Edited by L. Forrer and C. A. Hersh. 1952

Taylor, Lily Ross. **The Divinity of the Roman Emperor.** 1931

Two Studies on Roman Expansion: A. Afzelius. 1975

Two Studies on the Roman Lower Classes: M. E. Park and M. Maxey. 1975

Willems, P[ierre]. **Le Sénat De La République Romaine,** Sa Composition Et Ses Attributions. Three Volumes in Two. 1885/1883/1885